GINNY LOVE

simply Love
A Family Cookbook

HEDGEROW PRESS • 2008

Library and Archives Canada Cataloguing in Publication

Love, Ginny, 1962–
    Simply Love : a family cookbook / Ginny Love.
Includes index.
ISBN 978-0-9736882-7-6
    1. Cookery. I. Title.
TX714.L678 2008   641.5   C2008-904560-2

Published by
Hedgerow Press
P.O. Box 2471
Sidney, B.C. V8L 3Y3
hedgep@telus.net
www.hedgerowpress.com

Cover and text design: Frances Hunter

Printed and bound in Canada by Friesens

Contents

For my husband Gordon and our four wonderful children, Hamish, Cameron, Duncan and Maggie. They are my greatest supporters, invaluable critics and enthusiastic eaters.

And for my parents Cam and Terry Wilkinson, whose unfailing encouragement and support allowed me to pursue my love of cooking. When I was young, my dad spent countless early mornings on Salt Spring Island, loading the car with a table, patio umbrella and my baked goods for me to sell at the Saturday Market. My mum's dislike of cooking paved a smooth path for me to have free rein in our kitchen at home.

Introduction

Family Dinners

I've been cooking for almost all my life, sometimes professionally, sometimes just for fun and, now that we are a family of six, out of necessity.

Eating meals together is one of the most important features of our family life. I believe that family meals are not just about eating but about emotional and intellectual nourishment as well. When children sit at the dinner table with parents and adult relatives, they learn communication skills, build self-esteem as their interests are shared, and develop strong bonds with others.

There is evidence that families who eat together tend to eat better, with healthier diets that lead to healthier lifestyles. Miriam Weinstein documents a wide range of scientific studies to show that children and adolescents who regularly eat meals with their families achieve better grades in school, are less likely to develop eating disorders or abuse alcohol and drugs.[1]

In our fast-paced lives and with the lure of computers and video games distracting children, we have lost sight of the importance of family meals and their role in helping children develop into well-adjusted, healthy, socially responsible adults. When it comes to raising children, there are of course no guarantees, but serving regular healthy meals in a nurturing environment around a table, talking to one another, will have hugely positive results worth every effort involved.

When my children were small, the whole family could be together at the end of the day. Now they are older and their activities are pushed later in the day, not everyone can be home for dinner every night; those of us who are at home still have dinner together but some may have to eat earlier, some later. Sunday night, though, is still a family night, often including friends and grandparents.

Sometimes there's a child who doesn't think about or care about food. We have one of those children, Duncan. If he didn't have a meal put in front of him, it wouldn't occur to him to eat. He does just fine during the school year when he gets up, has breakfast and goes off to school with lunch in hand. At the end

of the day there is always dinner on the table, or something to heat up if he is not home at dinner time. During the holidays, however, things are different. He may sleep until 11 a.m. or noon, have breakfast, then miss lunch completely and even dinner if he is off golfing or busy with another activity.

I think it is our job as parents to make sure this kind of child does eat, and eat well. Duncan has always preferred fruit and vegetables to meat and potatoes, and he could live on Caesar salad. As he gets older he may have an increased interest in food. Until then we just have to keep reminding him to eat by putting food in front of him.

Plan now to bring your family back to the dinner table. Start small and try for one night a week. Set the table, turn off the TV and let the machine answer the phone. For working parents with smaller children, weekends might be best for a family meal night; for families with teenagers, a weeknight would be a better option.

I have been interested in cooking from the time when, at about age twelve, I started selling my baked goods at the now-famous Saturday market on Salt Spring Island. Some of my most popular recipes from those days are included in this book.

Love of food led me to cooking school at the Cordon Bleu in London and classes at La Varenne when I was living in Paris. When I returned to Vancouver, I joined one of the top caterers in the city, working in all areas of the business.

In 1987 I went into business for myself and opened *The Cooking Company Café and Restaurant* on Vancouver's West Broadway. For five fun and successful years, my business partner Jennifer and I prepared and served delicious, wholesome, home-cooked food to hundreds of happy customers. We didn't work with a set menu but were inspired by whatever fresh ingredients were available to us at the beginning of the day.

Much like running a restaurant, cooking for a family requires the basic ingredients, proper equipment, a little planning and some great recipes. Sure, my cooking background makes meal preparation easier for me, but meals need not be complicated. Family meals should be easy to prepare: in this book you will find many simple recipes for every day. The priority should not be time spent in the kitchen but time together as a family.

1. *The Surprising Power of Family Meals: How Eating Together Makes Us Smarter, Stronger, Healthier and Happier* (Steerforth Press, 2005).

School Lunches

I have never met anyone who "loves" to make school lunches. Personally, I look forward to the end of June for its two-month break from the bagged lunch chore. The only problem is that all through the summer the kitchen is a mess all day, with people coming and going, eating at different times. As the end of August arrives, I actually look forward to getting the first two meals of the day finished up by

8.15 a.m. Back to school is like a new year, with a fresh start on school lunches.

I have a friend whose three school-aged children make their own lunches after dinner the evening before. It's a great idea as it ensures everyone prepares what they want, but I've never been organized enough to do it.

Obviously there is no point in packing foods your children don't like. My four kids have different food preferences: some like mayonnaise in their sandwiches, some don't; some like yellow mustard, others want honey mustard. It makes for more work to cater to their tastes but it prevents waste.

Friends who have worked as supervision aids in elementary schools tell me they see large quantities of food tossed into the garbage, with hundreds of apples thrown away. If it turns out your children haven't eaten fruit at school, make sure they have some when they get home. I love mandarin orange season because this easy-to-peel fruit is popular with everyone.

Four things go in my lunch kits: a sandwich or wrap, or some kind of main dish; fruit or vegetables; a drink; and a treat or sweet.

Choose various kinds of breads and buns for sandwiches; cold pizza is an option. If you shop at the beginning of the week, you can buy enough sliced meats to last the week. Leftovers or soups can be heated up and put in a wide-mouth Thermos.

Iceberg lettuce, tomatoes and cucumber can be sliced and kept in sealed containers in the fridge, easy to pull out as you make the sandwiches.

When baking cookies or squares, I make a double batch so I can wrap several in plastic wrap to keep in the freezer, easy to pull out for the lunch kits as needed. These are much healthier than store-bought treats, with way less packaging. Many schools don't allow nuts in lunches as some children suffer allergic reactions to them; it's best to avoid these altogether, as well as peanut butter.

Sending a lunch to school is healthier and less expensive than the alternatives. Children don't always make the wisest choices from what is available in or near their schools. It is expensive to buy lunch every day and you can prepare a lunch at home for a fraction of the price. Having said that, I usually let my kids buy lunch in high school or get a hot lunch in elementary school once a week. It's a break from routine and gives them something different to look forward to. The important thing is to make sure children eat a good nutritious lunch as often as possible.

My Kitchen Tools

Like every cook, I can spend hours browsing through kitchen shops. I love looking at the gadgets and equipment but have learned from experience that I don't need them all and wouldn't use them if I bought them. My kitchen tools are quite simple and easily stored.

SAUCEPANS

- Two 12-inch skillets, one with a tight-fitting lid
- Three heavy, cast iron-coated Dutch ovens (Mine are Le Creuset)
- Pots and pans of various sizes (choose types suitable for your stove top)

UTENSILS KEPT NEXT TO THE STOVE

- Knife block with good quality sharp knives
- Assortment of wooden and metal spoons, rubber or silicone spatulas in various sizes, tongs, whisk, scissors, ladle

UTENSILS IN DRAWER

- Can opener, garlic press, vegetable peeler, zester, cheese grater, pastry cutter, rolling pin, silicone pastry brushes, ice cream scoop, bottle opener, meat thermometer, potato ricer

EQUIPMENT IN CUPBOARDS

- Stainless steel bowls in many sizes; they fit into one another
- Stainless steel colander

- Cake pans and loaf tins in various sizes
- Glass baking dishes in various sizes (useful for casseroles as well as cakes and squares)
- Two sets of measuring cups, one glass set for liquids, one stainless steel for dry measures
- Handheld electric blender with small food processor attachment with metal blade (useful for chopping ginger, garlic and small amounts of nuts)
- Chopping boards
- Mandoline (see page 47)

ON THE COUNTER OR SHELF

- Stand-up food processor
- Electric mixer
- Toaster
- Slow cooker
- Rice cooker
- Waffle iron

appetizers

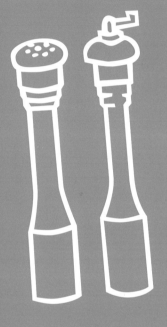

Our everyday family meals don't usually begin with an appetizer. However, when we have guests it's always nice to offer a few nibbles before dinner. The appetizers here are all simple to prepare and can be made ahead of time.

I like to put out a plate of fresh vegetables to munch on, either with or without dip. A deep glass filled with long carrot sticks is colourful and healthy. If you keep a jar of pepper jelly in your pantry or fridge then you can always use it on top of crackers with cream cheese.

Cheese Biscuits

Makes about 8 dozen biscuits

My mum has been making these biscuits for years. You can split the recipe in half if you like, but they freeze very well in an airtight container and are great to have on hand for unexpected guests or for an after-school snack. As a variation, add 1 tablespoon (15 mL) chopped fresh rosemary.

1 pound (500 grams) sharp Cheddar cheese, grated
2½ cups (625 mL) flour
1 teaspoon (5 mL) salt
½ teaspoon (2 mL) dry mustard
1 cup (250 mL) soft butter
¼ teaspoon (1 mL) cayenne

1 egg white, lightly beaten
1 to 2 tablespoons (15 to 30 mL) sesame seeds

Combine first six ingredients in the bowl of an electric mixer. Stop the machine when the mixture begins to come together. Divide the mixture in half and roll it into 2 separate logs each about 10 inches (25 cm) long. Wrap each log in wax paper and chill at least 4 hours or up to 2 days.

Preheat oven to 350F (180C). Line baking sheets with parchment paper. Slice the biscuits thinly, about ⅛ inch (.4 cm) thick. Arrange on baking sheets. They don't spread much so they can be placed quite close together. Brush a little beaten egg white in the centre of each biscuit and sprinkle a pinch of sesame seeds on top.

Bake 12 to 15 minutes. The biscuits should be golden brown around the edges so they stay crisp. Cool on racks.

BUTTER – Although recipes from other cooks often call for unsalted butter, I prefer regular salted butter. I buy it in large quantities and keep it in the freezer. If you prefer to use unsalted butter, slightly increase the amount of salt specified in my recipes.

Asparagus with Wasabi Mayonnaise

Serves 10 to 15

I prefer to use the fatter spears of asparagus for this appetizer.

2 pounds (1 kilogram) asparagus

WASABI MAYONNAISE

¾ cup (180 mL) mayonnaise
2 teaspoons (10 mL) soy sauce

½ teaspoon (2 mL) sugar
2 teaspoons (10 mL) lemon or lime juice
2 teaspoons (10 mL) wasabi paste

Break off the tough bottom parts of the asparagus stalks. Bring a large pot of water to the boil. Have a large bowl of ice water ready. Plunge the asparagus into the boiling water and blanch for 1 minute. Drain and immediately immerse in the ice water. When the asparagus is cool, drain on paper towel or a clean tea towel.

Combine the ingredients for the wasabi mayonnaise. Pour into a small serving bowl. Arrange the asparagus on a plate with the wasabi mayonnaise on the side.

Pesto and Sundried Tomato Torta

Serves 10 to 20

Here is another make-ahead appetizer. The recipe comes from my cousin (in-law) Kara, who brings it to every family get-together. She is expert at making it. Be sure to spread the pesto and sundried tomatoes right to the edges of the bowl so that the layers can be seen when the torta is unmoulded. Serve with crackers or sliced baguette.

8 ounces (250 grams) spreadable
   cream cheese
½ cup (125 mL) butter, at room temperature
¼ cup (60 mL) finely chopped Spanish
   (mild) onion

½ cup (125 mL) pesto sauce (see page 110)
½ cup (125 mL) chopped sundried tomatoes
½ cup (125 mL) toasted pine nuts
Fresh basil for garnish

Using an electric mixer or a food processor, blend together the cream cheese and butter until smooth. Add onion and mix to blend.

Line a 2-cup (500 mL) bowl with plastic wrap. Spread one-third of the cream cheese mixture on the bottom. Layer half of the pesto over the cheese, making sure you get it right to the edges. Spread half the chopped sundried tomatoes over the pesto. Add a second layer of cheese, using half of the remaining mixture. Spread remaining pesto over cheese, then the remaining sundried tomatoes over the pesto. Spread the remaining cheese mixture over the top. Wrap the torta well and refrigerate for at least 2 hours or overnight.

Just before serving, unmould onto a serving plate. Press toasted pine nuts onto the surface. Garnish with fresh basil and arrange crackers or sliced baguette around the outside of the dish.

Sundried Tomato and Goat Cheese Spread

Makes about 1½ cups

This appetizer is easy to mix up in a food processor. My kids have always loved it, but I never tell them it has goat cheese in it. Serve on plain water crackers. The fresh rosemary is really important. If the recipe makes more than you need, freeze half to use at a later date.

1 clove garlic
6 to 8 sundried tomatoes, packed in oil
1 tablespoon (15 mL) chopped fresh rosemary
2 – 6-ounce (170 grams) packages plain goat cheese,
   at room temperature
6 ounces (170 grams) cream cheese, at room temperature

Fit food processor with a metal blade. While the motor is running drop the garlic through the feed tube and chop finely. Stop the machine and add the sundried tomatoes and chopped rosemary. Pulse on and off to mince the tomatoes. Add the goat cheese and cream cheese; process until smooth. Transfer the spread to 1 or 2 small serving dishes. This spread freezes very well.

Baked Bacon and Cheese Triangles

Makes about 70 to 80 triangles

This is a tasty hot appetizer you can make well in advance and freeze, ready to pull out of the freezer and pop in the oven when you have unexpected guests. If you are having a cocktail party, prepare these at least a week in advance so you are not doing everything on the last day.

1 pound (500 grams) bacon, sliced into ¼ inch (.5 cm) pieces
1 large onion, finely chopped
3 cups (750 mL) grated sharp white Cheddar cheese
1 cup (250 mL) sliced almonds
Freshly ground pepper
½ cup (125 mL) mayonnaise

Five (9- or 10-inch/23 or 25 cm) flour tortillas

Fry the bacon until crisp in a large skillet on medium heat. Transfer to paper towel to drain fat and cool. Drain off all but 1 tablespoon (15 mL) of the bacon fat from the skillet. Sauté the onions over medium heat until soft, about 5 to 7 minutes. Transfer to a medium bowl. Cool 10 to 15 minutes. Add the crisp bacon, grated cheese, almonds, pepper and mayonnaise to onions. Gently stir all the ingredients together. Lay the tortilla shells out on the counter. Divide the filling among the five tortillas and, using a metal spatula, spread evenly, making sure you get all the way to the outside edges. Cut the tortilla shells into random shapes that are about 1½ to 2 inches (3 to 5 cm) big. Lay the pieces on a baking sheet lined with wax paper, putting layers of wax paper between the tortillas. Cover with plastic wrap and freeze for several hours. If you are using them at a later date, stack them in a cookie tin or covered plastic container and freeze until ready to serve.

To bake tortillas, preheat oven to 375F (190C). Lay the tortilla pieces in a single layer on a baking sheet. Bake until cheese is melted and edges are golden, 5 to 7 minutes. Cool slightly before serving.

Judy's Guacamole

Serves 10 to 15

It took a long time to get this guacamole recipe from my neighbour Judy. The joke on the street was that you could send ripe avocados over to her house and they would come back as guacamole. My kids were constantly asking me to make it. One day Cameron took the ripe avocados across the street, along with a recipe card and a pen. He watched her make guacamole and wrote everything down. This is now one of Cameron's signature recipes.

1 or 2 cloves garlic
1 large green onion
quarter of a small tomato
3 or 4 pickled jalapeño slices
2 to 3 tablespoons (30 to 45 mL)
    fresh lemon juice
½ teaspoon (2 mL) salt
3 large or 5 small ripe avocados

Tortilla chips

Using the small processor attachment of a handheld blender, combine garlic, green onion, tomato, jalapeño slices, lemon juice and salt. Pulse the mixture until it becomes smooth.

Working quickly so that the avocados don't brown, cut them in half and twist to open. Holding the avocado half in the palm of your hand, tap the blade of the knife onto the pit and gently twist it to remove the pit. Reserve 1 or 2 avocado pits for the serving bowl (they help keep the avocado from turning brown). Using a wet soupspoon, scoop the avocado flesh from the skin and place it all in a medium-sized bowl. Mash the avocado, using a pastry cutter or fork. Add the tomato mixture and mix well. Taste to see if it needs more salt. Pile the guacamole on top of the avocado pits. It is best to serve guacamole quickly after making, but you can wrap it tightly with plastic wrap and refrigerate until ready to serve. Serve with tortilla chips: I like the whole grain ones because they have more flavour.

Seven Layer Mexican Dip

Serves 10 to 20

Make this appetizer the day it is served or the avocado will turn brown. Serve on a platter surrounded with large tortilla chips. Leave the small broken chips in the bag!

1 – 19-ounce (540 mL) can refried beans
   with jalapeños
2 large avocados
1 tablespoon (15 mL) lemon juice
½ teaspoon (2 mL) salt
3 drops hot sauce
1 cup (250 mL) sour cream
1 cup (250 mL) grated Cheddar cheese
1 cup (250 mL) grated Monterey Jack cheese
½ cup (125 mL) chopped green onions
1 – 4-ounce (113 gram) can sliced black olives
   (about ⅓ cup/75 mL)
1 large or 2 medium tomatoes
1 to 2 bags tortilla chips

Spread the refried beans evenly over the bottom of a 10-inch (25 cm) glass pie plate. Cut open the avocados and remove the pits. Spoon the pulp into a small bowl and mash with a fork or a pastry cutter. Add the lemon juice, salt and hot sauce. Spread the avocado mixture evenly over the refried beans. Stir up the sour cream to soften it a bit. Drop the sour cream by spoonfuls over the top of the avocado and then spread evenly. Sprinkle cheeses over the sour cream. Sprinkle green onions and black olives over the cheeses. Quarter the tomatoes and with your fingers remove as much of the pulp as you can. Finely dice the tomatoes and sprinkle over all. Wrap and chill until ready to serve.

A PASTRY CUTTER keeps warm hands off the butter in pastry making. It is also useful for mashing such things as avocados, bananas and hard-boiled eggs.

soups

At The Cooking Company *we served two freshly made soups every day, with a slice of cheese bread (recipe on page 30). In making soups you can let your imagination run wild by combining any suitable ingredients you have in your kitchen.*

A hearty soup, with some veggie sticks, cheese and bread, makes an excellent weekday meal.

Cream of Celery Soup

Makes about 12 cups (3 L)

Young children like this soup because of its mild flavour and creamy texture that comes from milk, not cream. It is important to peel the celery.

SOUP BASE

1 large head of celery
2 medium or 1 large onion, chopped
2 tablespoons (30 mL) butter
2 cloves garlic, mashed
6 to 8 cups (1.5 to 2 L) vegetable or chicken broth

WHITE SAUCE

3 tablespoons (45 mL) butter
3 tablespoons (45 mL) flour
3 cups (750 mL) low-fat milk

Salt and freshly ground pepper

To make the soup base, cut the bottom off the celery and trim off the leafy tops. Take each individual stalk and run a vegetable peeler down the back of it to remove the stringy bits: this gives the soup a nice consistency. When you have peeled all the stalks, rinse them under cold water. Chop the celery into ¾-inch (1.5 cm) pieces.

Melt the butter in a large heavy pot. Add the celery and onions. Cook over medium heat until softened without browning, about 5 to 10 minutes. Add the mashed garlic and cook an additional minute. Add just enough broth to cover the vegetables. Turn the heat up and bring to a boil. As soon as it boils, turn it down to simmer and cook about 30 minutes.

Meanwhile in a medium-sized heavy saucepan make the white sauce by melting 3 tablespoons (45 mL) butter over medium heat. Add the flour and cook for about a minute. Add the milk and stir constantly until it comes to a boil. Turn the heat down to low and cook, stirring often, for about five minutes.

When the soup base is cooked, purée it in a blender or use a handheld blender. Be sure to get out all the lumps. Combine the celery mixture and the white sauce. Check for seasoning, adding salt and pepper if needed.

Asparagus and Leek Soup

Makes about 12 cups (3 L)

Adding a potato to this soup gives it a creamy texture without any cream.

3 large leeks
2 medium onions, chopped
2 tablespoons (30 mL) butter
2 cloves garlic, mashed
2 bunches asparagus (about 1½ pounds/
    750 grams)

8 cups (2 L) vegetable or chicken broth
1 medium Russet potato, peeled and
    chopped into ½-inch (1 cm) dice
Salt and freshly ground pepper

Cut the dark green parts off the leeks. Slice them in half vertically down the middle. Chop in ½ inch (1 cm) pieces. Put all the leeks in a colander and rinse well under cold running water until completely clean. Drain well.

Break the tough stems off the bottom of the asparagus and discard. Cut stalks into 1 inch (2 cm) pieces. Rinse well. In a large pot, melt butter, add leeks and onions. Cook over medium heat without browning for 5 to 10 minutes. Add the garlic and cook 1 minute more. Add the asparagus, broth and potato. Cook the soup until all the vegetables are tender, about 30 minutes. Cool.

Purée the soup in a blender or use a handheld blender. Taste for seasoning, adding salt and pepper if needed.

Lentil Soup

Makes about 10 cups (2.5 L)

Try this soup out on your kids: I was surprised to find that mine liked it.
Soup also makes a great school lunch packed in a Thermos.

2 tablespoons (30 mL) olive oil
4 carrots, peeled and chopped
4 stalks celery, peeled and chopped
2 onions, chopped
2 cloves garlic, mashed
1 teaspoon (5 mL) ground cumin

¾ cup (175 mL) de Puy (French) lentils or
    green lentils
6 cups (1.5 mL) vegetable or chicken broth
¾ cup (175 mL) tomato sauce or
    1 – 28-ounce (796 mL) can of tomatoes,
    puréed with a handheld blender
Salt and freshly ground pepper

Heat oil in a large pot. Sauté carrots, celery and onions for about 10 minutes on medium heat until soft, stirring often. Don't let them brown. Add garlic and cumin and cook 1 minute more. Add lentils, broth and tomato sauce or tomatoes. Bring to a boil, turn down heat and simmer about 45 minutes. Add more broth if you like a thinner soup. Season with salt and pepper.

Minestrone Soup

Makes about 12 cups (3 L)

This soup makes a perfect winter meal, served with bread and cheese and a veggie tray.

2 to 3 tablespoons (30 to 45 mL) olive oil
2 medium onions, chopped
4 carrots, peeled and chopped
4 stalks celery, peeled and chopped
2 cloves garlic, mashed
8 cups (2 L) chicken or vegetable broth
1 – 28-ounce (796 mL) can tomatoes, puréed in
    a blender or with handheld blender
½ teaspoon (2 mL) basil
½ teaspoon (2 mL) oregano
½ cup (125 mL) pasta, any small shape
1 cup (250 mL) canned red kidney beans, rinsed
Salt and freshly ground pepper

In a large heavy pot heat the olive oil over medium heat. Add the onions, carrots and celery. Cook, stirring occasionally, for 5 to 7 minutes. Add the garlic and cook 1 minute more. Add broth, tomatoes, basil and oregano and bring to a boil. Add the pasta; turn the heat down to low and simmer 20 to 30 minutes. Add the kidney beans and heat another 5 minutes. Taste for seasoning, adding salt and pepper if needed.

You can make homemade broth if you like, but I just use the Tetrapak broths readily available in grocery stores. They are always there in the pantry and any leftovers will keep in the fridge for up to 2 weeks. On the tops I mark the date I opened them before putting them in the fridge.

Beef Barley Soup

Makes about 12 cups (3 L)

It has become a Halloween tradition in our family to have Beef Barley Soup before the kids go trick-or-treating. They are always excited and so busy getting ready that sitting down to eat would be next to impossible. I make the soup early in the day so I have my hands free for last-minute make-up and costume adjustments. Some sliced bread and a cheese plate are all you need to complete this meal.

1½ pounds (750 grams) lean ground beef
1 large onion, diced
3 or 4 carrots, peeled and chopped
4 stalks celery, peeled and chopped
1 red or green pepper, chopped
2 cloves garlic, mashed
1 – 28-ounce (796 mL) can whole or diced tomatoes
6 cups (1.5 L) beef broth
1 teaspoon (5 mL) dried oregano
1 teaspoon (5 mL) dried basil
½ teaspoon (2 mL) freshly ground pepper
1 or 2 teaspoons (5 to 10 mL) salt
⅓ cup (75 mL) pearl barley

In a large heavy pot cook the beef over medium heat, breaking it up with a spoon, until no longer pink. Add the onion, carrots, celery and red or green pepper. Cook 5 to 7 minutes more, until vegetables are soft. Add the mashed garlic and cook 1 minute more. You can add diced tomatoes to the pot right out of the can but whole tomatoes should be puréed first with a handheld blender. Add the tomatoes, broth, oregano, basil, pepper, salt and barley to the soup. Bring to a boil and turn down to simmer. Cook the soup until the barley is tender, 30 or 40 minutes. Taste for seasoning and add more salt if necessary. If you like a thinner soup, add some more broth.

My handheld blender is one of my favourite kitchen tools: I use it for many things including puréeing tomatoes right in the can.

Spicy Tomato Soup

Makes about 10 cups (2.5L)

With cans of tomatoes in your pantry, you can make this soup in a few minutes. If you prefer a tomato cream soup, add white sauce when the soup is cooked.

2 tablespoons (30 mL) olive oil
2 onions, chopped
2 medium carrots, peeled and diced finely
1 stalk celery, peeled and diced finely
2 cloves garlic, mashed
2 – 28-ounce (796 mL) cans plum tomatoes,
    puréed with a handheld blender
4 cups (1 L) vegetable or chicken broth
2 teaspoons (10 mL) sugar
¼ teaspoon (1 mL) hot sauce
1 teaspoon (5 mL) dried basil
1 teaspoon (5 mL) dried oregano
Salt and freshly ground pepper

Heat olive oil in a large heavy pot. Add onions, carrots and celery and cook until vegetables are soft without browning, 5 to 10 minutes. Add garlic and cook 1 to 2 minutes more. Add tomatoes, broth, sugar, hot sauce, basil and oregano. Bring soup to a boil, turn down the heat and simmer for about 30 minutes. Taste and adjust seasoning as needed.

WHITE SAUCE FOR TOMATO CREAM SOUP

2 tablespoons (30 mL) butter
2 tablespoons (30 mL) flour
2 cups (500 mL) milk

In a medium saucepan melt butter over medium heat. Add flour and cook 1 minute. Add milk, stirring constantly. Bring sauce to the simmer and cook 2 or 3 minutes, stirring constantly. Add the sauce to the soup and stir well. Adjust seasoning.

I always have canned tomatoes in my pantry, either whole or diced. I purée the tomatoes with a handheld blender before adding them to the soup. Crushed canned tomatoes do not work well because they are too thick and dry for most of the recipes.

Corn Chowder

Makes about 12 cups (3 L)

*This is a hearty soup. You can use any combination of vegetables,
whatever is in your fridge. The amount of salt you add in the end will
depend upon what broth you use. Some have more salt than others.*

1 pound (500 grams) bacon, sliced
    into ½-inch (1 cm) pieces
¼ cup (60 mL) butter
2 medium onions, chopped
4 stalks celery, chopped
4 carrots, peeled and chopped
1 red pepper, chopped

2 cloves garlic, mashed
¼ cup (60 mL) flour
8 cups (2 L) chicken broth
2 cups (500 mL) frozen corn
1 large potato, peeled and chopped
    in ¼-inch (.5 cm) dice
Salt and freshly ground pepper

Cook bacon in a large heavy pot over medium heat
until very crisp. Remove with slotted spoon and drain
on paper towel. Discard all but 1 tablespoon (15 mL)
of the bacon fat. Add butter to pot and melt. Add
onions, celery, carrots and red pepper. Sauté until
soft, 5 to 10 minutes. Add garlic; cook 1 minute. Add
flour and cook 1 minute more. Add broth and bring
to boil. Add potato and corn, bring back to boil and
simmer until potato is cooked, 20 to 30 minutes.
Return bacon to soup. Season with salt and pepper.

Split Pea Soup

Makes about 10 cups (2.5 L)

*When I was young, my mother floated chopped European wieners
or hot dogs in the Split Pea Soup. It made the soup more appealing
to kids and I loved it. You can use up leftover ham by chopping it and
adding it to the soup after it is cooked. If you prefer a vegetarian soup,
there is no need to add any meat at all.*

2 cups (500 mL) split peas, green or yellow
   or a combination of the two
1 large onion, chopped
2 large carrots, peeled and chopped
3 stalks celery, peeled and chopped
1 clove garlic, mashed

8 cups (2 L) vegetable or chicken broth
1 bay leaf
Salt and freshly ground pepper
1½ cups (375 mL) chopped ham or
   3 or 4 European wieners, chopped
   (optional)

Rinse the split peas in a colander and put them in a large heavy pot.
Add the onion, carrots, celery, garlic, broth and bay leaf. Bring the soup
to a boil. Turn down heat to simmer and cook the soup for about 1 hour.
Let the soup cool before puréeing. Remove the bay leaf. The soup can be
puréed in batches in a blender or with a handheld blender right in the pot.
Taste for seasoning. Reheat soup with chopped ham or wieners if desired.

Mulligatawny Soup

Makes about 12 cups (3 L)

This curried chicken and rice soup was very popular at The Cooking
Company. *If you haven't already introduced brown rice to your children,
this is a good place to start. It will be hidden in the soup but will add
some nutrition. Remember to peel the stringy bits off the back of the
celery before chopping it.*

2 tablespoons (30 mL) butter
1 large onion, chopped
2 or 3 carrots, peeled and chopped
2 or 3 stalks celery, peeled and chopped
1 red or green pepper, chopped
1 or 2 cloves garlic, mashed
1 teaspoon (5 mL) curry powder

2 tablespoons (30 mL) flour
8 cups (2 L) chicken broth
2 cups (500 mL) chopped chicken
   or turkey meat
½ cup (125 mL) rice
Salt and freshly ground pepper

Melt butter and sauté vegetables in a large heavy pot on medium heat
for 5 to 10 minutes until soft but not brown. Add garlic and cook 1 minute
more. Add curry and flour; cook another minute, stirring constantly.

Add broth and rice, bring to boil. Turn down to low and add chicken.
Cook soup about 45 minutes on low heat. Season with salt and pepper.

Vegetable Potage

Makes about 10 cups (2.5 L)

On our first family trip to Europe I was nine years old. I have a few food memories from that trip and, not being a very adventurous eater in those days, I encountered some disasters. Luckily it was France and "steak and frites" were on most menus. Ketchup was a bit harder to come by!

I remember eating a "potage" in a hotel restaurant near Cap d'Antibes and I loved it. A potage is a thick puréed soup. When I make a potage at home I use any combination of vegetables that need to be used up. It's a great way to get vegetables into unsuspecting kids.

2 tablespoons (30 mL) butter
2 medium onions, chopped
2 leeks, white and light green part only,
   chopped and washed well
2 cloves garlic, mashed
5 or 6 carrots, peeled and chopped
4 stalks celery, peeled and chopped
1 small zucchini, chopped
1 Russet potato, peeled and cut in ½ inch (1 cm) cubes
8 cups (2 L) vegetable broth
1 bunch spinach, washed and chopped coarsely
Salt and freshly ground pepper

In a large saucepan, melt butter, add onions and leeks. Cook over medium heat without browning, about 5 or 10 minutes. Add garlic, carrot, celery, zucchini, potato and broth. Bring to boil, turn down heat and cook soup about 30 minutes until vegetables are tender. Add spinach and cook for a few minutes until it is wilted. Cool. Purée the soup with a blender or a handheld blender until smooth. Add salt and pepper if needed. Reheat gently in saucepan, stirring frequently.

Butternut Squash, Parsnip and Apple Soup

Makes about 12 cups (3 L)

The sweetness of the apple in this soup makes it appealing to everyone.

3 tablespoons (45 mL) butter
2 medium onions, chopped
2 leeks, white and light green part, sliced and washed
½ teaspoon (2 mL) ground nutmeg
2 butternut squash (about 3½ pounds/1.75 kg total)
    peeled, seeded and chopped
1 large or 2 small parsnips, peeled and chopped
1 Granny Smith apple, peeled, cored and chopped
6 cups (1.5 L) vegetable broth
1½ cups (750 mL) apple juice
Salt and freshly ground pepper
Sour cream for garnish

Melt butter in a large heavy pot over medium heat. Add onions and leeks; cook 5 to 7 minutes until soft. Add the nutmeg; cook an additional 1 or 2 minutes. Add squash, parsnip, apple, broth and apple juice. Bring the mixture to a boil, turn heat down to low and cook about 45 minutes until the squash is soft. Cool. Purée the soup in batches in a blender or use a handheld blender to purée it in the pot before reheating. Season the soup with salt and pepper. When serving the soup, garnish with a dollop of sour cream and some freshly grated nutmeg if desired.

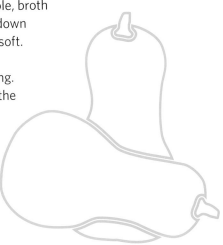

Chicken Noodle Soup

Makes about 16 cups (4 L)

Everybody loves homemade Chicken Noodle Soup. I just buy cooked rôtisserie chickens from the grocery store. They are easy to pull apart and chop up. If you don't have any broth you can use water and some bouillon cubes or packets. Taste the soup before you add salt; it may not need any. Use any kind of pasta. Egg noodles are not very dense so 2 cups (500 mL) is just the right amount. If you use broken-up spaghetti, you would only need about ¾ to 1 cup (175 to 250 mL). Substitute any herbs if you don't like thyme and dill.

1 large onion, chopped
4 or 5 carrots, chopped
3 or 4 stalks celery, chopped
1 red pepper, chopped
2 tablespoons (30 mL) olive oil
2 cloves garlic, mashed
12 cups (3 L) chicken broth
2 cups (500 mL) medium-wide egg noodles
3 cups (750 mL) chopped cooked chicken
¼ cup (60 mL) chopped fresh parsley
½ teaspoon (2 mL) dried thyme
½ teaspoon (2 mL) dried dill
Salt and freshly ground pepper

In a large pot cook the onions, carrots, celery and red pepper in the olive oil over medium heat for about 5 minutes. Add the garlic and cook for 1 or 2 minutes more. Add the broth and bring the soup to a boil. Add the pasta, chicken, parsley, thyme, dill, salt and pepper. Simmer soup until pasta is cooked. Taste for seasoning.

Broccoli Cheddar Soup

Makes about 12 cups (3 L)

This is another Cooking Company *recipe. Be sure to use the entire broccoli. Once you have cut off the flowerets, peel the stalk and cut it into chunks to add to the soup. The stalks are full of flavour and vitamins.*

¼ cup (60 mL) butter
3 onions, chopped
2 stalks celery, peeled and chopped
2 carrots, peeled and chopped
3 cloves garlic, mashed
1 large Russet potato, peeled and diced
3 bunches broccoli, cut up (about 2½ pounds/
   1.25 kg)
8 cups (2 L) chicken or vegetable broth
1 pound (500 grams) sharp Cheddar cheese,
   grated
Salt and freshly ground pepper

Melt butter in large heavy pot. Add onions, celery and carrots; cook slowly to develop flavour for about 10 minutes. Add garlic and cook 2 or 3 minutes. Add potato, broccoli and broth. Bring to boil, then turn heat down to medium-low and simmer about 30 minutes. Remove from heat. Cool. Blend with a handheld blender or use a regular blender. Return to pot. Add Cheddar cheese and stir to melt. Taste for seasoning. Do not boil soup with cheese in it or the cheese will separate.

SALT — I use coarse or kosher salt for all my cooking and baking. Because kosher salt is not iodized and usually has no additives, it lends a cleaner flavour to foods. If you prefer regular table salt, you might want to cut down the amount called for in the recipes. I keep both a small salt cellar and a pepper grinder right beside my stove.

Cheese Bread for Soup

Makes 1 – 8 x 4 inch (20 x 10 cm) loaf

*This bread does not have yeast in it, so it does not need to rise.
You can make up a batch quickly while your soup is simmering.
At* The Cooking Company *we baked many loaves of this cheese
bread every morning.*

2 cups (500 mL) flour
2 teaspoons (10 mL) baking powder
1 teaspoon (5 mL) baking soda
½ teaspoon (2 mL) salt
1 cup (250 mL) grated sharp
   Cheddar cheese
1 egg
¾ cup (175 mL) buttermilk

Preheat oven to 350F (180C). Butter the loaf pan.

In a large bowl combine flour, baking powder, baking
soda, salt and cheese. In another bowl beat the egg and
add the buttermilk. Pour buttermilk mixture over flour
mixture. Combine well and knead lightly. Place the dough
in the loaf pan. Bake the loaf for 30 to 40 minutes until
golden on top and hollow-sounding when you give it a tap.

salads

We all know we should eat lots of fruits and vegetables. Getting children to eat them can sometimes be a problem. You may find that if kids don't like cooked veggies they will eat them raw, cut up for their school lunches, put out as an after-school snack, or in salads. I love salad myself and make one for dinner almost every day.

Asian Cabbage Salad

Serves 8

This salad is so nice because it can be made well in advance and kids really enjoy it. Don't tell them it's made with cabbage! Leftovers are delicious the next day.

1 – 3-ounce (100 gram) package chicken or regular
    flavoured ramen soup noodles with seasoning mix
2 tablespoons (30 mL) butter
¾ cup (175 mL) slivered almonds
1 large Napa cabbage (suey choy)
1 bunch green onions, chopped
1 red bell pepper, chopped
2 large carrots, grated

DRESSING
¾ cup (175 mL) sunflower oil
⅓ cup (75 mL) red wine vinegar
1 garlic clove, mashed
1 tablespoon (15 mL) soy sauce
3 tablespoons (45 mL) sugar or
    2 tablespoons (30 mL) honey

With a rolling pin or the palm of your hand hit the package of noodles to break them up. Melt butter in a skillet and sauté broken noodles and seasoning mix with almonds over low heat, stirring often until golden, about 5 to 10 minutes. Cool completely.

Slice cabbage thinly and put in large bowl with green onions, red pepper and carrots.

Make dressing by combining oil, vinegar, garlic, soy sauce and sugar or honey in a small jar. Close the jar with a lid and shake vigorously to combine.

To serve, add noodles, nuts and about half the dressing to the vegetables and combine well. Salad can be tossed about 1 hour ahead of time. Store leftovers in a covered container in the refrigerator for up to 1 day.

Make salad dressings in large quantities and keep them in the fridge in jars with tight-fitting lids. You don't want to bother with making a different dressing every night. Washed lettuce should last for several days in the fridge if it is dried well and sealed in a bag along with a piece of paper towel.

Arugula Salad with Parmesan Cheese

Serves 6

Arugula is a small-leafed salad green with a spicy flavour. In England arugula is called "rocket" and when we were there with the children we ate a lot of "Rocket Salad". It is simple to make at home. Mix the arugula with some lettuce if you find the flavour too strong.

5 ounces (140 grams) baby arugula
⅓ cup (75 mL) freshly shaved Parmesan cheese
1 to 2 tablespoons (15 to 30 mL) cream of balsamic
3 to 4 tablespoons (45 to 60 mL) olive oil
Salt and freshly ground pepper

Toss the arugula in a salad bowl. Using a cheese slicer, slice large shavings of cheese into the salad bowl. If you don't have a slicer, simply grate the cheese. Just before serving toss the salad with the cream of balsamic, oil and salt and pepper.

Cream of balsamic is a condensed, slightly sweet, balsamic vinegar available at most grocery stores. For this salad use a good quality olive oil; you will taste the difference.

Fresh Corn and Tomato Salad

Serves 6

This salad is simple and delicious. You can make it all summer long when the corn is fresh. It's great for picnics and potlucks. I learned to make this salad from my friend Christine who visits every summer from Italy. Her cooking style is a constant reminder to me of how simple food preparation should be.

6 to 8 cobs of fresh corn
2 cups (500 mL) cherry or grape tomatoes
½ cup (125 mL) chopped fresh basil
½ teaspoon (2 mL) salt
Freshly ground pepper
3 tablespoons (45 mL) olive oil

Husk the corn and cook it in boiling salted water for about 4 minutes. Remove from the water and cool. Remove the corn from the cobs with a sharp knife. Transfer to a bowl. Add the tomatoes, basil, salt, pepper and oil. Stir and chill. You can make this salad several hours before serving.

Chopped Salad

Serves 6 to 8

I love to eat salad, but I don't always enjoy making it. Salad is usually the last thing I put together as I am preparing dinner but this salad can be made earlier in the day and all you have to do is toss it just before serving. Add whichever vegetables your family likes. Iceberg lettuce may not be the most nutritious, but kids really seem to like it. Any dressing also works well. Hamish came up with this dressing recipe and in his opinion it is the best ever!

SALAD

½ head iceberg lettuce, chopped
   (about 3 cups/750 mL)
½ head romaine lettuce, sliced thinly
   and washed (about 3 cups/750 mL)
¾ cup (175 mL) diced cucumber
¾ cup (175 mL) grated carrot
¾ cup (175 mL) chopped red pepper
¾ cup (175 mL) chopped mushrooms
¾ cup (175 mL) chopped tomatoes
½ cup (125 mL) chopped green onion
1 cup (250 mL) croutons (optional)
1 avocado, diced

DRESSING

3 tablespoons (45 mL) wine vinegar
1 tablespoon (15 mL) Dijon mustard
1 tablespoon (15 mL) honey
¼ teaspoon (1 mL) hot sauce
½ cup (125 mL) olive oil
Salt and freshly ground pepper

Place the lettuce in the bottom of a bowl. Add the cucumber, carrot, red pepper, mushrooms, tomatoes and green onion but do not toss. Cover the bowl and refrigerate until serving.

Prepare the dressing by combining the wine vinegar, mustard, honey and hot sauce in a small bowl. Whisk in the olive oil and season with salt and pepper.

Just before serving, add the avocado and croutons if using. Toss the salad and serve.

Orange & Feta Salad with Maple Dressing

Serves 6

Substitute pomegranate seeds for the oranges when they are in season. Make extra maple dressing to have available in the fridge.

DRESSING
⅔ cup (150 mL) olive oil
3 tablespoons (45 mL) red wine vinegar
¼ cup (60 mL) maple syrup
2 teaspoons (10 mL) Dijon mustard
½ teaspoon (2 mL) oregano

SALAD
¼ cup (60 mL) pine nuts, toasted
1 can (284 mL) orange segments, well drained
½ cup (125 mL) crumbled feta cheese

1 small head romaine lettuce, sliced and washed
1 small head red lettuce (washed and torn) or salad mix

To prepare dressing, mix together oil, vinegar, maple syrup, mustard and oregano using a handheld blender for a creamy texture. If you prefer, you can just shake them together in a jar.

Place lettuce in a salad bowl. Add nuts, oranges or pomegranate, and feta cheese. Just before serving, toss salad with enough dressing to coat the lettuce.

Greek Salad

Serves 6 to 8

This is a perfect salad to take to a potluck. You can chop all the vegetables, pour the oil and vinegar over top and cover and refrigerate for several hours before tossing and serving.

1 long English cucumber, partially peeled, quartered lengthwise and chopped into ½-inch (1 cm) pieces
2 tomatoes, cut into chunks
1 red pepper, cut in chunks
1 green pepper, cut in chunks
1 yellow pepper, cut in chunks

1 small red onion, diced fine
¾ cup (175 mL) crumbled feta cheese
½ cup (125 mL) calamata olives
1 teaspoon (5 mL) dried or 2 teaspoons (10 mL) chopped fresh oregano
Freshly ground pepper
2 tablespoons (30 mL) balsamic vinegar
4 tablespoons (60 mL) olive oil

Place the cucumber, tomatoes, red pepper, green pepper, yellow pepper and onion in a salad bowl. Sprinkle the feta cheese, olives, oregano and pepper over top. Pour olive oil and vinegar over salad. Cover and refrigerate until ready to serve. Toss gently before serving.

Summer Cabbage Slaw

Serves 8 to 10

This is a nice light slaw recipe, perfect for summer barbecues. It is also wonderful the next day. Prepare the vegetables early in the day and toss the dressing over the salad just before serving. For a picnic, toss the salad before you leave home.

SALAD
2 cobs corn
1 small head green cabbage
2 carrots, peeled and grated
1 small red onion, sliced thinly
   or chopped
1 red pepper, thinly sliced

DRESSING
¼ cup (60 mL) frozen orange juice
   concentrate, thawed
¼ cup (60 mL) sunflower oil
¼ cup (60 mL) rice vinegar or
   apple cider vinegar
¾ teaspoon (4 mL) salt
Freshly ground pepper

Husk the corn and boil it for about 4 minutes. Cool while you prepare the remaining vegetables and dressing. Remove the outside leaves of the cabbage. Quarter and core it. Slice the cabbage thinly with a sharp knife or slicing blade of a food processor and place it in a large bowl. Add the grated carrots. Add the red onion and sliced red pepper to the bowl. Cut the corn off the cob and add to the salad. If you are preparing the salad early in the day, cover and chill.

To prepare the dressing, whisk together the orange juice concentrate, oil, vinegar and salt. Pour the dressing over the salad and toss well. Transfer to a serving bowl.

Caesar Salad with Balsamic Dressing

Serves 6

*This simple Caesar Salad recipe is a favourite in our house. It omits
anchovies, because I find that children generally don't like their taste.
I also don't like to put egg in salad dressings so I use mayonnaise instead.
Sometimes I toss some chopped avocado and crisp bacon pieces into
the salad.*

1 large head romaine lettuce, washed and dried

DRESSING

1 to 2 cloves garlic
3 tablespoons (45 mL) lemon juice
3 tablespoons (45 mL) balsamic vinegar
¼ cup (60 mL) grated Parmesan cheese
1 tablespoon (15 mL) Dijon mustard
1 teaspoon (5 mL) Worcestershire sauce
⅓ cup (75 mL) mayonnaise
½ cup (125 mL) olive oil
¼ teaspoon (1 mL) salt
¼ teaspoon (1 mL) freshly ground pepper

CROUTONS

2 tablespoons (30 mL) olive oil
1 tablespoon (15 mL) butter
2 cups (500 mL) cubed day-old bread
Salt and freshly ground pepper

Make the croutons. In a large skillet, melt the oil and butter over medium
heat. Add the bread cubes, stirring well to coat with butter and oil. Season
with salt and pepper. Turn the heat down to low and continue to cook the
croutons, stirring frequently until crisp, 10 to 15 minutes.

Make the dressing in a food processor fitted with a metal blade. With
the motor running, drop the garlic through the feed tube to mince. Stop
the machine and add the lemon juice, balsamic vinegar, Parmesan cheese,
mustard, Worcestershire sauce and mayonnaise. Mix well. With the motor
running, slowly pour the oil through the feed tube. Add salt and pepper.
Transfer the dressing to a jar with a tight-fitting lid.

Tear the lettuce into a bowl. Add croutons and half the dressing. Toss
well just before serving. The extra dressing can be stored in a jar in the
fridge for up to 2 weeks.

Green Salad with Candied Almonds and Orange Balsamic Dressing   Serves 6

I usually double or triple this dressing recipe as it keeps for several weeks in the fridge. Everyone seems to love a salad with the crunch of nuts and the sweetness of fruit.

CANDIED ALMONDS
¾ cup (175 mL) slivered almonds
2 tablespoons (30 mL) sugar

DRESSING
2 tablespoons (30 mL) balsamic vinegar
¼ cup (60 mL) orange juice
1 tablespoon (15 mL) Dijon mustard
1 clove garlic, mashed
¼ teaspoon (1 mL) salt
¼ teaspoon (1 mL) freshly ground pepper
⅔ cup (150 mL) olive oil

SALAD
1 head of red or green leaf lettuce, washed and dried, or 1 package of mixed baby greens or a combination of the two
1 avocado, diced
1 – 10-ounce (284 mL) can orange segments, well drained or 1 orange, peeled and chopped
⅓ cup (75 mL) finely diced red onion

For the candied almonds, combine almonds and sugar in a small non-stick skillet. Cook over medium heat, stirring constantly with a wooden spoon, until the sugar melts and the almonds become a dark golden brown. Transfer to a plate to cool and harden.

To prepare the dressing, combine vinegar, orange juice, mustard, garlic, salt, pepper and oil in a jar, cover with lid and shake well. Or use a handheld blender or a blender to produce a creamier, emulsified dressing.

Combine lettuce, avocado, oranges and red onion. Break up nuts over salad. Toss with dressing just before serving.

OLIVE OIL — I keep two kinds of olive oil in the pantry (not in the fridge, where it would coagulate). I buy large containers of a cheaper one to use for sautéeing and in salad dressings and one bottle of really good quality olive oil to mix with balsamic vinegar for dipping fresh bread into at the table. It's healthier than butter and children love dipping their bread.

Spinach Salad with Mango Chutney Dressing

Serves 6

I never would have dreamed of putting all these things in a salad for children. My friend Liz introduced this salad to us and I was surprised that the kids actually loved it. You can mix spinach with other lettuces in this easy salad. The bean sprouts add a nice crunch.

SALAD

8 slices bacon, cut in ½-inch (1 cm) long slices
3 ounces (90 grams) Gruyère cheese, grated
1 cup (250 mL) bean sprouts
½ small red onion, chopped or sliced thinly
1½ cups (375 mL) sliced mushrooms
1 avocado, sliced
2 large bunches or 1 large bag spinach

MANGO CHUTNEY DRESSING

2 teaspoons (10 mL) Dijon mustard
1 glove garlic, mashed
2 tablespoons (30 mL) mango chutney
3 tablespoons (45 mL) red wine vinegar
¾ cup (175 mL) olive oil

To prepare the dressing, combine the mustard, garlic, chutney, vinegar and olive oil in a blender or with a handheld blender.

To prepare the salad, cook the bacon over medium heat until very crisp. Drain on paper towel and cool. Up to 1 hour before serving, combine the bacon, cheese, bean sprouts, onion, mushrooms and avocado in the bottom of a salad bowl. Pour half the dressing over top and toss to coat. Just before serving, add spinach to salad bowl and toss the salad, adding some more dressing if needed.

Couscous Salad

Serves 6

Couscous is a Middle Eastern pasta made from coarsely ground durum wheat. It has very little taste, so you can do what you wish with it. Use this recipe as a guide for quantities, because you can add anything you like: grated carrots, chopped celery or chopped peppers. It is a nice salad to bring to a potluck because it can be made well in advance. Leftovers last two or three days.

1 cup (250 mL) couscous
1 cup (250 mL) water
1 teaspoon (5 mL) salt
2 lemons
1 clove garlic, mashed
½ teaspoon (2 mL) sugar
Salt and freshly ground pepper
½ cup (125 mL) olive oil
½ cup (125 mL) chopped parsley
½ long English cucumber, ¼-inch (.5 cm) dice
2 medium tomatoes, seeded and cut into
   ¼-inch (.5 cm) dice
3 to 4 green onions, chopped

For some dishes, like this couscous salad, you don't need all the seeds and juice from the tomatoes. It is easy to remove most of them by quartering the tomato and pulling out the juice and seeds with your fingers.

Bring water and salt to a boil in a saucepan. As soon as it boils, turn off heat, add the couscous and stir briefly. Place lid on saucepan and let it sit for five minutes. Fluff the couscous with a fork, transfer it to a bowl and let cool about 15 minutes.

Meanwhile combine the dressing ingredients. Squeeze the juice from the lemons into a small bowl and add the garlic, sugar, salt and pepper. Slowly whisk in the olive oil.

Add parsley, cucumber, tomatoes, green onions and vinaigrette to the cooled couscous. Stir well. Add more salt and pepper if necessary.

Potato Salad

Serves 6

This is a traditional potato salad with no peeling required.
If you don't like eggs leave them out.

2 pounds (1 kg) small Yukon Gold or red potatoes
1 tablespoon (15 mL) salt
3 tablespoons (45 mL) dill pickle juice
¼ cup (60 mL) chopped red onion
4 green onions, chopped
¾ cup (175 mL) chopped celery
½ cup (125 mL) chopped dill pickles
¼ cup (60 mL) chopped parsley
3 hard-boiled eggs, coarsely chopped
Salt to taste

DRESSING

½ cup (125 mL) mayonnaise
3 tablespoons (45 mL) sour cream
2 teaspoons (10 mL) Dijon mustard
½ teaspoon (2 mL) freshly ground pepper
½ teaspoon (2 mL) sugar

Cut the potatoes in uniform-sized pieces, about ¾-inch (1.5 cm) chunks. Bring a large pot of water to a boil and add salt. When the water boils add the potatoes. Watch them carefully so as not to overcook them. They will take less than five minutes, but err on the side of undercooked as they will continue to cook a bit as they cool. Drain and place in a large bowl. Add the pickle juice and stir gently. Cool.

To prepare the dressing, combine the mayonnaise, sour cream, mustard, pepper and sugar. When the potatoes are cool mix in the red onion, green onions, celery, pickles and parsley. Stir in the eggs and the dressing. Season with salt and chill until ready to serve. Can be made several hours ahead of time and even a day ahead, kept cool in the fridge.

vegetables

Many families struggle with the problem of getting their children to eat enough vegetables, or any vegetables at all for that matter. I am a strong believer in putting out a tray of raw cut-up veggies (and dip if you like) well before dinner. Any leftovers can be brought to the table. This works especially well for young children. If you really can't get them to eat any vegetables, be sure that they have some fruit in their diet. Many of the vegetable and potato dishes in this chapter can be made ahead and reheated; this makes last minute dinner preparation much easier.

Asparagus with Lemon Shallot Dressing

Serves 8 to 10

This dressing goes well over sliced tomatoes as well as asparagus. Prepare a platter of both when you are feeding a crowd in the summer. You can prepare the vegetables and dressing early in the day and pour the dressing over top just before serving.

2 large bunches of asparagus, about 2 pounds (1 kg)

DRESSING

Juice of 2 lemons
1 teaspoon (5 mL) Dijon mustard
½ teaspoon (2 mL) salt
¼ teaspoon (1 mL) freshly ground pepper
½ teaspoon (2 mL) sugar
1 shallot, finely chopped
½ cup (125 mL) olive oil
½ cup (125 mL) sunflower oil

To blanch asparagus, using both hands bend the asparagus spear and break it where it wants to snap; then bring a pot of salted water to a boil. Immerse the asparagus and cook 1 to 3 minutes, depending on the thickness of the stalk. Have a large bowl of ice water ready. Drain the asparagus and quickly immerse in the ice water to stop the cooking process and preserve the colour. When completely cooled, drain on a clean tea towel and arrange on a platter.

To make the dressing, combine the lemon juice, Dijon mustard, salt, pepper, sugar, shallot, olive oil and sunflower oil in a jar with a tight-fitting lid. Shake well.

Drizzle dressing over asparagus just before serving.

Glazed Carrots

Serves 6

These carrots go well with any meal. For a big family dinner, make them early in the day and keep them in the fridge until ready to heat and serve. Even kids who are not wild about vegetables like these glazed carrots.

8 to 10 medium-sized carrots
1½ tablespoons (22 mL) butter
1½ teaspoons (7 mL) Dijon mustard

1½ tablespoons (22 mL) brown sugar
¼ teaspoon (1 mL) salt

Peel the carrots and slice them on the diagonal into ½-inch (1 cm) slices. Steam them over boiling water until just tender, about 5 minutes. Drain in a colander and rinse with cold water to stop the cooking process.

Meanwhile, melt the butter in the saucepan. Add the Dijon mustard and brown sugar and cook over low heat for 1 or 2 minutes until incorporated. Return the carrots to the pan, add salt and stir to glaze the carrots. If you are serving them immediately, heat the carrots in the glaze.

If making them ahead, transfer the glazed carrots to a microwave-safe dish and cool. Cover and refrigerate until ready to serve. Heat the carrots for four or five minutes in the microwave, or in a saucepan until heated through.

Braised Red Cabbage

Serves 8 to 10

Not every kid loves this dish, but I sometimes add it to the list of veggies for a large family dinner. My German friend Heidi taught me to make this, using a few tricks to make it really special. It is wonderful with pork or pot roast, not only for its taste but because its colour is spectacular. One of the things that makes it so good is stirring in something sweet at the end of the cooking. Prepare this dish well in advance, even a day ahead, and reheat it in the pot you cook it in. I use my food processor to slice the cabbage but you can also use a sharp knife or a mandoline.

2 tablespoons (30 mL) butter
1 medium onion, chopped
1 head red cabbage, cored and sliced thinly
1 green apple, peeled, cored and chopped
1 bay leaf
2 to 3 tablespoons (30 to 45 mL)
    wine vinegar or cider vinegar
2 to 3 tablespoons (30 to 45 mL)
    brown sugar
Pinch of cloves
½ teaspoon (2 mL) salt
¼ teaspoon (1 mL) freshly ground pepper
1 to 2 tablespoons (15 to 30 mL) jam or
    plum sauce

In a large heavy saucepan, melt the butter
and add the onion. Cook onion until soft.
Add the cabbage, apple and bay leaf. Cook
cabbage mixture over low to medium-low
heat for about 30 minutes. Add 2 tablespoons
(30 mL) of the vinegar, 2 tablespoons (30 mL)
of the sugar and the cloves, salt and pepper.
Cook cabbage for another 30 minutes, remove
bay leaf and adjust seasoning. Add remaining
vinegar and sugar if needed. Add jam or plum
sauce. Add more salt and pepper if needed.

If making ahead, cook for 1 hour the day
before or earlier in the day and reheat in the
same pot over low heat for another half hour
before serving.

A MANDOLINE is a slicing device consisting of a metal blade and two parallel boards, one fixed and one adjustable in height. Some versions have several interchangeable blades. The object to be sliced is pulled along the top of the board and through the blade, resulting in uniform slices which can be much thinner than hand-slicing can achieve.

Scalloped Potatoes

Serves 8 to 10

Scalloped potatoes are traditionally made with cream. You can make a dish equally as tasty using milk in a very thin white (béchamel) sauce. This dish can be made ahead, partially baked and reheated the next day. The potatoes can be sliced by hand or with the slicing blade of a food processor. I have an inexpensive mandoline which works really well for this.

¾ pound (400 grams) sharp Cheddar cheese, grated
1 medium onion, sliced thinly
3 tablespoons (45 mL) butter

3 tablespoons (45 mL) flour
4 cups (1 L) low-fat milk
5 to 6 large Russet potatoes
Salt and freshly ground pepper

Preheat oven to 350F (180C). Butter a 13 x 9 x 2-inch (3.5 L) ovenproof dish. Have the cheese ready in a small bowl. Have the onion ready in another bowl. Melt the butter in a medium-sized heavy saucepan over medium heat. Add the flour and cook 1 to 2 minutes without browning. Add the milk and cook, stirring constantly, over medium heat until the mixture comes to a boil. Turn heat down to low, adding ½ teaspoon (2 mL) salt and ¼ teaspoon (1 mL) pepper. Cook about five minutes and turn off the heat. Peel the potatoes and slice them thinly using a food processor, a knife or a mandoline.

Layer a quarter of the potato slices on the bottom of the pan. Sprinkle them with a quarter of the onions, a quarter of the cheese and some salt and pepper. Ladle a quarter of the sauce over top. Repeat these layers 3 more times, sprinkling the top with cheese. Bake in preheated oven 45 to 55 minutes.

To bake the potatoes in advance, cook them for about 40 minutes, remove from oven, cool, cover with parchment and then foil; refrigerate until ready to reheat. They will need another 40 to 50 minutes at 375F (190C) before serving. Take the parchment and foil off for the last 15 minutes to brown the top.

Ratatouille

Serves 10 to 12

Ratatouille is a Mediterranean vegetable stew. It may not be a favourite with children, but it is a great dish for entertaining in any season and can be served hot or cold.

In the summer, ratatouille can be put out on the buffet table along with any barbecued meat and salads. Serve it cold with some feta cheese crumbled over top.

I used to make large pots of ratatouille for our local community meal. As I am always looking for shortcuts, I discovered then that I didn't need to sauté the vegetables. I just chop them all up, add the canned tomatoes and spices and turn on the heat. This dish is full of goodness and has no fat at all.

1 small eggplant, partially peeled and
    cut in ¾-inch (1.5 cm) dice
½ teaspoon (2 mL) salt
1 large onion, large dice
1 red pepper, large dice
1 green pepper, large dice
1 yellow pepper, large dice
1 medium zucchini, large dice
8 large mushrooms, stemmed and quartered
2 cloves garlic, mashed

1 – 28 ounce (796 mL) can diced tomatoes
3 tablespoons (45 mL) tomato paste
1 teaspoon (5 mL) sugar
1 teaspoon (5 mL) dried oregano
1 teaspoon (5 mL) salt
½ teaspoon (2 mL) freshly ground pepper
¼ teaspoon (1 mL) hot sauce
1½ cups (375 mL) crumbled feta cheese or
    ¾ cup (175 mL) freshly grated Parmesan
cheese

Place the diced eggplant in a colander and sprinkle with salt. Toss to coat and let sit 5 to 10 minutes to remove the eggplant's bitter after-taste. Rinse under cold water and drain well.

Place all the eggplant, onion, red pepper, green pepper, yellow pepper, zucchini, mushrooms, garlic, canned tomatoes, tomato paste, sugar, oregano, salt, pepper and hot sauce in a large heavy pot with a lid. Set the heat to low and stir frequently. It may not seem like much liquid, but as the vegetables cook, they will produce lots of juices. As the ratatouille becomes juicier, after about 20 minutes, remove the lid and turn up the heat to medium. Cook for about 20 minutes more. Check for seasoning. Serve hot or cold sprinkled with cheese.

Gratin of Root Vegetables

Serves 12 to 15

This is a very rich dish for a special occasion but you only need a small serving. It is such a good addition to Christmas dinner because it can be made well in advance and is wonderful for leftovers on Boxing Day.

2 tablespoons (30 mL) butter
3 or 4 large leeks
1½ cups (375 mL) whipping cream
1 cup (250 mL) light cream
1 teaspoon (5 mL) dried sage or
    2 teaspoons (10 mL) fresh
1 teaspoon (5 mL) dried rosemary or
    2 teaspoons (10 mL) fresh

1 tablespoon (15 mL) Dijon mustard
1 teaspoon (5 mL) salt
½ teaspoon (2 mL) freshly ground pepper
4 or 5 large parsnips
2 or 3 yams (about 1½ lbs/750 grams)
⅓ cup (75 mL) grated Parmesan cheese
½ cup (125 mL) grated Gruyère cheese

Preheat oven to 400F (200C). Butter a 13 x 9 x 2-inch (3.5 L) baking dish. Slice the dark green parts off the leeks on an angle so that they resemble a sharp pencil. Cut off the root end and slice the leek in half lengthwise. Slice in ¼-inch (.5 cm) pieces. Place in colander and rinse very well, separating all the pieces. Drain well.

In a large bowl whisk together the whipping cream, light cream, sage, rosemary, mustard, salt and pepper.

Melt the butter in a large sauté pan. Add the leeks and cook on medium heat until soft but not brown. Transfer to the bowl with the cream mixture.

Peel the parsnips and slice into ¼-inch (.5 cm) rounds. Peel the yams and slice into ¼ inch (.5 cm) rounds. Bring a large pot of salted water to a boil. Cook the parsnips and yams together until almost tender, 3 to 5 minutes. Drain well. Add to bowl with leeks and cream. Stir gently and transfer to prepared baking pan. Sprinkle cheeses over top. Butter a piece of foil and cover the gratin. Bake in preheated oven for about 30 minutes. Remove foil and continue to bake another 30 minutes or so until cheese is golden and gratin is set and bubbly. Let gratin sit for about 10 minutes before serving.

To make this dish 1 or 2 days ahead, remove from oven after 30 minutes and cool to room temperature. Cover and refrigerate 1 to 2 days. On serving day return gratin to 350F (180C) oven for 45 to 60 minutes. Remove foil after about 30 minutes to brown the top.

Make-Ahead Mashed Potatoes Serves 8

In recent years, potato ricers have regained popularity. My mum has had one since she was married so I adopted it. It gives the potatoes such a fine texture. If you don't have a ricer, use an electric handbeater or a handmasher. For a special occasion like Christmas, you can substitute light cream for the milk.

6 large Russet potatoes
   (about 4½ pounds/2.5 kg)
2 teaspoons (10 mL) salt
½ cup (125 mL) butter

¾ cup (175 mL) milk
¼ cup (60 mL) sour cream
1 teaspoon (5 mL) salt
¼ teaspoon (1 mL) ground white pepper

Peel the potatoes and cut them in quarters. Place them in a saucepan and cover with cold water. Add 2 teaspoons (10 mL) salt to the cooking water. Bring the potatoes to a boil, turn down the heat and simmer about 20 minutes until they are tender when poked with a knife.

Drain the potatoes well and return them to the pot. Shake them over medium heat for a few seconds to dry them out. Press the potatoes through a ricer into a bowl; alternatively, mix them with an electric mixer or mash them with a hand-masher. Melt the butter in the microwave or in a small sauce-pan. Add the milk and heat for another 40 seconds or so to warm the milk. Add the warm liquid to the potatoes, stirring well. Check for seasoning and add salt and white pepper. Stir in the sour cream. If you are serving the potatoes within the hour, place them in a stainless steel bowl, cover them with parchment paper and set the bowl over a pot of simmering water.

If making the potatoes ahead of time, transfer them to a shallow buttered ovenproof dish and cover them with parchment paper, then with foil. Cool to room temperature before refrigerating or freezing. Reheat the potatoes at 325F (160C) for 45 to 60 minutes covered. If frozen be sure to thaw them in the fridge for 2 days before reheating.

When making mashed potatoes, drain the potatoes over a bowl and reserve some of the potato juice for gravy. Let the juice sit for about 10 minutes. Pour off some of the watery top and reserve the starchier part from the bottom of the bowl. You can freeze this potato water for making gravy later.

Seasoned Potato Wedges

Serves 6 to 8

These potatoes are cooked at high heat, which makes them crispy on the outside and perfectly cooked on the inside. You can use Yukon Gold potatoes instead of Russet. Since they are smaller you will need about 8 to 10 of them. Buy a jar of ready-made seasoning salt, any type.

6 medium Russet potatoes
3 tablespoons (45 mL) olive oil
3 tablespoons (45 mL) butter
1 teaspoon (5 mL) seasoning salt

Preheat oven to 400F (200C). Turn on convection if you have it.

Scrub the potatoes. Cut them in half lengthwise and then each half in thirds lengthwise. Melt the butter, oil and salt together in the microwave or in a small saucepan. Combine potatoes and butter mixture in a large bowl. Transfer to a baking sheet, making sure they are in a single layer. Bake 20 to 30 minutes or until potatoes are golden and cooked through.

Lemon Potatoes

Serves 8 to 10

This tangy and delicious recipe is from my mother-in-law, Joan. It is a great dish to serve with Greek food or alongside any barbecued meats. The boiling water steams the potatoes and will cook off at the end. You can also use large Yukon Gold potatoes. If they are the size of a medium apple, just cut them in half. You don't have to peel them.

2 tablespoons (30 mL) butter
¼ cup (60 mL) olive oil
2 to 3 garlic cloves, mashed
½ cup (125 mL) fresh lemon juice
Salt and freshly ground pepper, about ½ teaspoon (2 mL) of each
7 large or 10 medium Russet potatoes
2 cups (500 mL) boiling water

Preheat oven to 400F (200C). Melt butter in the microwave or in a saucepan. Add olive oil, garlic, lemon juice and salt and pepper. Peel potatoes if desired and quarter lengthwise. Combine potatoes and lemon mixture in a large bowl. Place potatoes in a deep roasting pan; they should cover the bottom in a single layer and not be piled on top of one another. Pour boiling water over the potatoes and place pan in oven. Roast about 1 hour or until potatoes are brown on top and the water has evaporated. Keep your eye on them so that they don't dry out. If they are not cooked after 1 hour, turn the heat down to 350F (180C) and continue cooking for 10 to 15 minutes more.

Shaved Brussels Sprouts

Serves 8 to 10

For many people, it's not Christmas without Brussels sprouts. I know other people who call them "green grenades" and are happy to live without them. Shaving or slicing the Brussels sprouts gives them a completely different texture and taste.

2 pounds (1 kg) Brussels sprouts
2 tablespoons (30 mL) butter
4 large shallots, thinly sliced
2 tablespoons (30 mL) olive oil
2 tablespoons (30 ml) cream of balsamic
   or balsamic vinegar
Salt and pepper

Rinse the Brussels sprouts. Trim the stem and remove the outer leaves. Slice the sprouts as thinly as possible, using the slicing blade of a food processor or a sharp knife.

In a large skillet, melt the butter and add the shallots. Stir frequently over medium heat until the shallots are nice and brown. Add the olive oil and the Brussels sprouts to the pan. Continue to cook the sprouts, stirring often for about 5 to 7 minutes. Add the cream of balsamic or the balsamic vinegar. Season with salt and pepper and serve. They can be made ahead by chilling in a sealed container in the fridge. Reheat in a skillet over low heat for 5 to 10 minutes.

Spiced Roasted Potatoes

Serves 8 to 10

Once you get the proportions down, you can combine any mixture of spices to your taste. Turmeric gives the potatoes a lovely yellow colour.

5 to 6 large Russet potatoes
¼ cup (60 mL) sunflower oil
1 teaspoon (5 mL) ground cumin
1 teaspoon (5 mL) salt

½ teaspoon (2 mL) freshly ground pepper
½ teaspoon (2 mL) ground turmeric
½ teaspoon (2 mL) ground ginger
⅛ teaspoon (.5 mL) ground cloves

Preheat oven to 450F (230C). Use convection if you have it.

Combine the spices and set aside. Peel the potatoes and cut them into 1-inch (2.5 cm) chunks. Place them in a large bowl. Quickly pat them dry with a clean tea towel. Add the oil and spices and stir well. Spread them out over 2 baking sheets. The potatoes should be in a single layer and not piled on top of each other. Roast them for 25 to 35 minutes, tossing once or twice during cooking. If you have a convection oven, they will cook faster. If the potatoes are ready before the rest of the meal, transfer them to a serving dish and keep warm in a 200 to 250F (100 to 120C) oven.

Roasted Asparagus

Serves 6

For this dish, use asparagus with thicker stalks: they don't shrivel up when cooked.

1 pound (500 grams) asparagus
2 tablespoons (30 mL) olive oil
¼ teaspoon (1 mL) salt
3 tablespoons (45 mL) freshly grated Parmesan cheese

Preheat oven to 375F (190C). Break off the bottom of each stalk of asparagus. Rinse and dry. Lay asparagus on a baking sheet. Drizzle with olive oil and salt. Toss lightly to coat asparagus with oil. Roast 10 to 15 minutes until firm to fork. Remove pan from oven, sprinkle with Parmesan cheese and return to oven for 3 to 4 minutes to melt the cheese. Serve hot.

chicken

Chicken can be prepared in so many different ways; it's perfect for family meals because most people like it in some shape or form. Chicken pieces can be removed from the freezer in the morning and be thawed, ready to cook, in the afternoon.

African Chicken with Curry and Peanut Sauce

Serves 6 to 8

This is an ideal dish for slow cooking. Serve with jasmine rice made in the rice cooker. If you don't have a slow cooker, bake the chicken and sauce in a heavy pot or Dutch oven with a tight-fitting lid for 2 hours at 300F (150C).

12 chicken thighs, bone in, skin off
2 tablespoons (30 mL) vegetable oil
2 onions, chopped
1 red pepper, chopped
3 cloves garlic, mashed
1 teaspoon (5 mL) curry powder
2 tablespoons (30 mL) sherry
½ cup (125 mL) peanut butter
¾ cup (175 mL) tomato sauce
¾ cup (175 mL) chicken stock
1 teaspoon (5 mL) dried oregano
1 bay leaf
1 teaspoon (5 mL) salt
½ teaspoon (2 mL) freshly ground pepper

Heat the oil in a large skillet over medium-high heat and brown chicken thighs in 2 batches. Season chicken lightly with salt and pepper. Place in slow cooker.

Turn heat down to medium; add onions and red pepper and sauté until soft, about 10 minutes. Add garlic and curry powder, cook 1 minute more. Add sherry and scrape up browned bits from the bottom of the pan. Add peanut butter, tomato sauce, chicken stock, oregano, bay leaf and salt and pepper and bring to boil. Pour over chicken and cook in slow cooker, on high heat 4 hours or low heat for 6 to 8 hours.

SLOW COOKER — I use my slow cooker often during the winter months. It requires some thinking ahead, but there is nothing better than having dinner all ready by doing the prep in the morning or the night before. Place the filled slow cooker pot in the fridge overnight. Take it out in the morning and turn on the slow cooker. Your house will smell great all day.

Barbecued Beer Can Chicken   Serves 6 to 8

My husband Gordon loves beer, so this is the perfect recipe for him. It is fun to make and results in a moist and tasty dish. I always make two chickens. The leftovers are great cold, or you can take the meat off the bone and put it in a pasta salad.

2 – 3 to 4 pound (1.5 to 2 kg) whole chickens

RUB FOR CHICKEN

2 teaspoons (10 mL) salt
1 teaspoon (5 mL) freshly ground pepper
1 tablespoon (15 mL) brown sugar
1 tablespoon (15 mL) white sugar
1 teaspoon (5 mL) celery seed
½ teaspoon (2 mL) cayenne pepper

1 teaspoon (5 mL) mustard powder
½ teaspoon (2 mL) garlic powder
3 to 4 tablespoons (45 to 60 mL)
   chopped fresh herbs if available
   (rosemary, oregano, parsley, sage)

2 – 12-ounce (350 mL) cans beer
   at room temperature
More whole fresh herbs for beer cans

Rinse the chickens in cold water and pat dry. Prepare the rub by combining the salt, pepper, brown sugar, white sugar, celery seed, cayenne, mustard, garlic and chopped herbs. Sprinkle about 1 tablespoon (15 mL) rub on the inside of each chicken. Rub equal parts of remaining rub all over each chicken. Refrigerate until ready to cook.

Open both cans of beer. Pour about one-third of each can into a glass and chill for later consumption! Use a can opener to punch 2 more holes in the top of each can. Push the whole fresh herbs into each can.

Preheat the barbecue to high. Set the beer cans upright on the barbecue and lower the chicken cavities over the cans, using the chickens' legs as a tripod. If you have a middle grill turn that off and set the front and back (or side) grills to medium. Close the barbecue lid. Reduce the temperature of the barbecue to medium so that the temperature is at about 350F (180C). Without lifting the lid too much, let the chicken cook about 1½ hours or until the interior temperature of the chicken reaches 170F (77C). Be careful not to spill the hot beer when you take the chickens off the barbecue. Using large tongs, lift the chickens off the beer cans and set them on the carving board. Discard beer. Allow the chicken to stand for at least 10 minutes before carving.

Bombay Chicken

Serves 6 to 8

Zip chicken pieces into re-sealable bags the day before you want to serve them so the meat has time to absorb flavour. This chicken marinade has an Indian flavour but is not too spicy. You can either bake it in the oven or barbecue it. This is a great dish to prepare at home and take away for a weekend at a cabin.

½ cup (125 mL) mango chutney
½ cup (125 mL) soy sauce
¾ cup (175 mL) honey
1 tablespoon (15 mL) chopped ginger
2 cloves garlic, mashed
1 teaspoon (5 mL) curry powder
1 tablespoon (15 mL) lemon juice
2 to 4 drops hot sauce

8 to 10 chicken pieces, skin removed, bone in or out

To prepare the marinade, use a whisk or a handheld blender to combine the chutney, soy sauce, honey, ginger, garlic, curry powder, lemon juice and hot sauce. Place chicken pieces in 1 or 2 re-sealable bags and pour marinade over chicken. Seal bags and refrigerate for up to 1 day or at least 4 hours.

Preheat oven to 375F (190C). Place chicken in a single layer on a baking pan. Bake 45 to 60 minutes. Occasionally baste the chicken with the marinade.

If using a barbecue, preheat to high. Transfer the chicken pieces to the grill and cook covered about 5 minutes. Turn pieces and cook 5 minutes more. If possible, turn off the middle element and turn heat down to medium and continue to cook until done, about 20 minutes more.

Serve with basmati rice.

If you are unable to turn off one element to continue to cook the chicken over indirect heat, just turn the barbecue down to low heat.

Pistachio Chicken with Avocado Sauce

Serves 6

This easy dish is a crowd pleaser in our family. Using a food processor for the sauce gives it a very smooth texture. If you don't have a food processor you can mash the avocados with a fork or a pastry cutter and whisk in the other sauce ingredients.

1½ cups (375 mL) shelled pistachios, chopped medium
½ teaspoon (2 mL) salt
½ teaspoon (2 mL) freshly ground pepper
6 boneless skinless chicken breasts
½ cup (125 mL) buttermilk or regular milk
2 tablespoons (30 mL) olive oil

AVOCADO SAUCE

2 teaspoons (10 mL) grated onion
2 large ripe avocados
¼ cup (60 mL) olive oil
¼ cup (60 mL) fresh lime juice
Salt to taste

Preheat oven to 375F (190C). Place pistachios, salt and pepper in a shallow dish. Dip chicken into milk and then press into nuts. Heat 2 tablespoons olive oil in large skillet. Cook chicken 2 minutes per side or until golden brown. Transfer to an ovenproof baking pan along with any nuts left in the pan. Bake 30 to 40 minutes.

While the chicken is baking, prepare the avocado sauce by combining the onion, avocados, olive oil, lime juice, and salt in a food processor fitted with a metal blade. A handheld blender also works well. Serve sauce in a bowl on the side.

Chicken Wings with Ginger Soy Marinade

Serves 6

Children love chicken wings: maybe it is because they can eat them with their fingers.

This recipe is in my mum's repertoire. She makes them when we all go to Salt Spring Island for the weekend. When she first started serving them, the kids were growing quickly and their appetites were increasing. She could never buy enough wings. I remember one dinner when the boys were trying to steal wings off my dad's plate when he wasn't looking.

Marinate the wings all day or for 24 hours if possible.

MARINADE
½ cup (125 mL) sunflower oil
½ cup (125 mL) soy sauce
2 tablespoons (30 mL) brown sugar
2 tablespoons (30 mL) lemon juice
4 cloves garlic, mashed
3 tablespoons (45 mL) chopped ginger
2 teaspoons (10 mL) sesame oil
2 tablespoons (30 mL) rice vinegar

5 to 6 pounds (2.5 to 3 kg) chicken wings

Make the marinade by mixing together the oil, soy sauce, brown sugar, lemon juice, garlic, ginger, sesame oil and vinegar. Divide the wings between 2 large strong re-sealable bags. Pour half the marinade into each bag. Seal the bags, removing as much air as possible. Refrigerate.

Preheat oven to 400F (200C). Line 2 baking pans with foil to make clean-up easier. Drain excess marinade off wings. Spread the wings in a single layer over both baking pans. Bake 30 to 40 minutes until chicken wings are cooked through and browned. Serve hot or at room temperature.

Chicken Pot Pie

Serves 8 as 1 pie, or 4 from each of 2 smaller pies

Chicken Pot Pie can have any kind of pastry on top. Phyllo is easy to work with for people who dislike making pastry. You can also use frozen puff pastry or buy regular pastry. Even a biscuit or scone topping is good.

It is best to allow the filling to cool completely before covering it with the pastry. You can make this dish a day ahead and add the pastry shortly before baking. Add some mushrooms to the filling if your family likes them. Cook them separately from the other vegetables in some butter, salt and pepper. Use any combination of chicken pieces: I like to use both white and dark meat.

2 pounds (1 kg) boneless skinless chicken
Salt and freshly ground pepper
⅓ cup (75 mL) white wine

½ cup (125 mL) butter
2 medium or 1 large onion, chopped
3 to 4 carrots, peeled and chopped
3 stalks celery, chopped
2 cloves garlic, mashed
5 tablespoons (75 mL) flour

2 cups (500 mL) liquid (I use the cooking liquid from the chicken plus extra chicken broth or milk)
2 teaspoons (10 mL) grated lemon zest
Salt and freshly ground pepper
2 tablespoons (30 mL) chopped fresh parsley
½ cup (125 mL) frozen peas (optional)

5 sheets phyllo pastry

Preheat oven to 350F (180C). Place the chicken in a 13 x 9 x 2-inch (3.5 L) ovenproof pan, season with salt and pepper and pour wine over top. Cover with foil and bake about 40 minutes, or until chicken is cooked through. Cool, reserving cooking liquid.

Melt ¼ cup (60 mL) of the butter in a large heavy pot. Add onions, carrots and celery. Cook on medium to medium-low heat until soft, about 5 to 7 minutes. Add garlic and cook another minute. Add flour and cook 1 to 2 minutes. Add the cooking liquid, bring the mixture slowly to a boil, turn down heat and cook another 5 minutes. Season with lemon zest, salt and pepper. Remove from heat.

Chop chicken into bite-size pieces. Add to vegetable mixture along with the parsley and frozen peas. Stir well. Check for seasoning. Pour mixture into 1 or 2 shallow ovenproof pans, large enough to have the filling go almost to the top. Cool completely. Pie can be made a day ahead; cover and refrigerate overnight.

Melt the remaining ¼ cup (60 mL) butter. Cut phyllo pastry to the size that will fit the pan you are using. While you are working with the pastry, keep it covered with a damp towel. Lay 1 sheet of phyllo on top of the pie. Brush liberally with butter. Repeat until you have about 4 to 6 layers of pastry. Bake the pie in a preheated 350F (180C) oven 45 to 55 minutes until pastry is golden brown and filling is bubbly.

Pecan and Dijon-coated Chicken

Serves 6

This is a really simple dish, quick and easy to prepare.

6 boneless skinless chicken breasts
¼ cup (60 mL) Dijon mustard
¼ cup (60 mL) buttermilk
Salt and freshly ground pepper
1½ cups (375 mL) chopped toasted pecans

Preheat oven to 350F (180C). Combine mustard, buttermilk, salt and pepper in a large bowl. Add chicken and marinate in the refrigerator for as long as possible, about 1 to 4 hours. Remove chicken breasts from marinade one at a time and press into chopped pecans. Set onto baking pan. Bake 40 minutes until chicken is cooked through.

BUTTERMILK — I use buttermilk for savoury dishes as well as in many of my baking recipes. It can be used in recipes that call for sour cream or yogurt, decreasing the amount slightly to account for its thinner consistency. Similarly, instead of buttermilk you can mix yogurt or sour cream with regular milk.

Mild and Sweet Chicken Curry   Serves 6

This curry sauce is not spicy and the sweetness makes it more appealing to children. Substitute prawns or shrimp if you prefer. You can use any combination of vegetables in this dish. I usually make equal amounts of vegetables and chicken or shrimp. Serve this curry over basmati rice.

¼ cup (60 mL) butter
2 medium onions, chopped
3 to 4 carrots, peeled and diced
3 stalks celery, chopped
1 red or green pepper, diced
1 Granny Smith apple, cored, peeled and diced
2 to 3 cloves garlic, mashed

2 teaspoons (10 mL) curry powder
1 teaspoon (5 mL) ground cumin
¼ cup (60 mL) flour
3 cups (750 mL) chicken broth
½ banana, mashed or 1 heaping tablespoon (15 mL)
   plum sauce or jam
2 pounds (1 kg) boneless skinless chicken
   (breast and/or thighs) cut in
   1-inch (2 cm) cubes
2 tablespoons (30 mL) olive oil
Salt and freshly ground pepper

Cut up chicken and set aside in the fridge. Chop vegetables and apple. In a large heavy saucepan, melt the butter and add the onions, carrots, celery, pepper and apple. Cook on medium heat until soft but not brown, 5 to 10 minutes. Add garlic and cook 1 minute more.

Add the curry and cumin. Stir well and cook 1 minute. Add flour and cook 1 minute more. Add the chicken broth and bring the mixture to a simmer, stirring often so that it doesn't burn. Add the banana or jam. Season the sauce with salt and pepper if required. It will depend on the saltiness of your broth.

Stir-fry the chicken in the olive oil with salt and pepper until cooked through. Add the chicken to the curry sauce and taste for seasoning.

Stir-Fry Chicken with Rice

Serves 6

For this amount of stir-fry you will need 1½ to 2 cups (375 to 500 mL) raw rice, prepared in the rice cooker. Don't be afraid to mix brown and white varieties.

SAUCE

1½ cups (375 mL) chicken stock
3 tablespoons (45 mL) soy sauce
2 large cloves garlic, mashed
2 tablespoons (30 mL) finely chopped fresh ginger
1 teaspoon (5 mL) sesame oil
2 tablespoons (30 mL) black bean sauce
½ teaspoon (2 mL) hot sauce
1 tablespoon (15 mL) honey

2 tablespoons (30 mL) cornstarch
3 tablespoons (45 mL) water

2 pounds (1 kg) boneless skinless chicken, breast and thigh
3 tablespoons (45 mL) teriyaki sauce

3 tablespoons (45 mL) vegetable oil

2 to 3 carrots, peeled and sliced on diagonal
2 to 3 stalks celery, peeled and sliced on diagonal
1 red pepper, quartered and sliced
10 green beans, cut in 1-inch (2 cm) pieces or 1 bunch broccoli, cut in flowerets
1 medium onion, chopped

To prepare the sauce, combine the chicken stock, soy sauce, garlic, ginger, sesame oil, black bean sauce, hot sauce and honey in a small bowl and set aside. Combine cornstarch and water in a cup and set aside. Cut chicken into bite-size slices and combine in a bowl with teriyaki sauce. Cut up vegetables and set aside in another bowl.

Using a wok or a skillet, heat 1 tablespoon (15 mL) of the oil over medium-high heat and stir-fry vegetables for 2 to 3 minutes. Return to bowl. Heat remaining 2 tablespoons (30 mL) oil over high heat and add chicken. Leave it in the hot oil for 1 or 2 minutes before stirring to allow it to brown. Continue to cook chicken, stirring occasionally until it is cooked through. Return vegetables to wok with chicken. Add sauce ingredients and bring to a simmer. Stir in cornstarch mixture, bring back to a simmer and cook several minutes to heat through and thicken. Serve with rice or chow mein noodles.

Chicken with Dijon Mustard and Rosemary

Serves 12

If it is not barbecue season, you can bake this chicken in the oven on foil-lined baking pans. This recipe makes a fair amount of marinade; you can either cut the recipe in half or keep the extra in the fridge for a week or two. Use any combination of chicken meat. The quantities given here are for a variety of sizes and meat colour. The chicken pieces can easily be transported for a weekend away while they are marinating in re-sealable bags.

6 bone-in chicken breasts, skin removed
8 bone-in chicken thighs, skin removed
4 whole chicken legs, skin removed

FRESH ROSEMARY AND DIJON MARINADE

½ cup (125 mL) Dijon mustard
2 cloves garlic, mashed

¼ cup (60 mL) soy sauce
¼ cup (60 mL) red wine vinegar
½ cup (125 mL) olive oil
¼ cup (60 mL) chopped fresh rosemary
1 tablespoon (15 mL) sugar
½ teaspoon (2 mL) freshly ground pepper

Prepare the marinade by combining the mustard, garlic, soy sauce, vinegar, olive oil, rosemary, sugar and pepper in a bowl. Divide chicken pieces among large, strong, re-sealable bags. Divide marinade between the bags, seal and refrigerate. Alternatively, combine all the chicken and marinade in a large stainless steel bowl, cover and refrigerate. The chicken should marinate for at least 4 hours or up to 24 hours.

Heat barbecue to medium-high heat. Remove the chicken from marinade onto barbecue, shaking off any excess. Close the lid on the barbecue and turn heat down to medium. Don't open the barbecue for about 4 to 5 minutes to allow the chicken to have attractive grill lines and seal in the juices. After 4 to 5 minutes, turn the chicken. Cook the chicken for another 20 to 30 minutes, watching carefully and turning occasionally. If you can, turn off the middle burners once the chicken is browned and cook with the lid down over indirect heat. This way the barbecue acts more like an oven and the chicken won't burn.

For oven cooking, preheat to 375F (190C). Lay the chicken on foil-lined baking pans and bake for 45 to 50 minutes, testing to make sure the large pieces are done.

Sweet and Sour Baked Chicken   Serves 6

This chicken dish is so easy and everyone loves it. In his Grade 12 year my son Hamish and a friend were in charge of cooking for 15 people on a school ski trip. They made this chicken dish one night and it was a huge hit. While the chicken is cooking, put some rice on to cook and prepare your vegetables.

8 to 10 chicken pieces, bone in (breasts, thighs
   and legs), skin removed
½ cup (125 mL) flour
1 teaspoon (5 mL) salt
½ teaspoon (2 mL) freshly ground pepper
¼ cup (60 mL) vegetable oil
1 – 3-cup (750 mL) jar tomato sauce
3 tablespoons (45 mL) brown sugar
3 tablespoons (45 mL) wine vinegar
   or cider vinegar
½ teaspoon (2 mL) cinnamon

Preheat oven to 350F (180C). Combine the flour, salt and pepper in a shallow bowl or a plate. Heat about 2 tablespoons (30 mL) oil in a large skillet over medium to medium-high heat. Dredge the chicken in the flour and brown it in batches in the oil, about 4 minutes on each side. As the chicken browns, transfer it to 1 or 2 ovenproof shallow baking dishes that will hold all the chicken pieces in a single layer.

Pour the tomato sauce into a bowl. Add the brown sugar, vinegar and cinnamon. Spoon the sauce over the browned chicken pieces. Bake the chicken for 40 to 50 minutes until cooked through.

RICE COOKERS are great for busy families. Once the rice is cooked, it will stay warm until you are ready to eat. Measure rice and water in the proportions given on the rice package. Soak rice in cold water for 10 minutes, or rinse it under cold running water. Drain well. Put rice, water, a knob of butter and pinch of salt in the cooker and turn it on, as much as a couple of hours ahead of time. Simple!

Chicken Enchiladas

Serves 6 to 8

For a shortcut, use 1½ jars (1.1L) prepared tomato sauce but add the cumin to it. Some children may not like sauce on top of their enchiladas, so leave a few without sauce before heating. This is a great way to introduce some whole grains by using whole wheat tortillas.

2 whole boneless skinless chicken breasts

TOMATO SAUCE

1 large onion, chopped
2 tablespoons (30 mL) oil
2 cloves garlic, mashed
1 – 28-ounce (796 mL) can tomatoes
1 teaspoon (5 mL) sugar
1 teaspoon (5 mL) cumin
½ teaspoon (2 mL) salt
½ teaspoon (2 mL) oregano
½ teaspoon (2 mL) basil

1 red pepper, sliced thin
1 green pepper, sliced thin
1 medium onion, sliced thin
1 tablespoon (15 mL) butter
¼ teaspoon (1 mL) ground cumin

8 to 10 – 9-inch (23 cm) flour tortillas
1½ cups (375 mL) grated Cheddar
1½ cups (375 mL) grated Monterey Jack
½ cup (125 mL) sour cream

Place chicken in baking dish, cover with foil and cook at 350F (180C) for about 40 minutes or until meat is no longer pink inside. Cool before cutting into bite-size strips.

Make tomato sauce. Cook onion in oil until soft. Add garlic and cook 1 minute more. Purée the tomatoes in the can, using a hand-held blender. Add the tomatoes to the onions along with the sugar, 1 teaspoon cumin, salt, oregano and basil. Bring to boil, turn down heat and simmer 20 minutes.

Melt butter in a medium skillet. Sauté the peppers and onion in butter for 3 or 4 minutes. Add ¼ teaspoon cumin and stir well.

Butter 2 ovenproof 13 x 9 x 2-inch (3.5 L) baking pans. Put about ¾ cup (175 mL) tomato sauce in each pan. Fill each tortilla with 2 tablespoons (30 mL) tomato sauce, ¼ cup (60 mL) chicken, some sautéed peppers and onions and 3 tablespoons (45 mL) grated cheese. Roll up and lay seam side down in the baking pan. Mix sour cream with remaining tomato sauce and spread over enchiladas. Top with remaining grated cheese. Heat at 350F (180C) for 30 to 40 minutes.

You could substitute 1 whole roasted chicken, meat removed and shredded, for the chicken breasts.

meat

From good old-fashioned Roast Beef and Yorkshire Pudding to simple Beef Lettuce Wrap, meat dishes are favourites with many families. They offer variety for family meals as well as for easy entertaining.

Risotto with Sausage

Serves 6

Last summer when we were traveling in Italy as a family we had dinner one night at the home of some friends just outside Verona. We were served a lovely risotto with some local sausage in it. The kids loved that meal and of course the risotto was just the first course!

Risotto is an easy weeknight dinner. The broth needs to be added slowly and the risotto has to be stirred constantly. It will only take about 20 minutes. Have one of your children stir the risotto while you are preparing the salad.

4 to 5 large sausages
1 large onion, chopped
2 cloves garlic, mashed
3 tablespoons (45 mL) olive oil
2 cups (500 mL) Arborio rice

½ cup (125 mL) white wine
8 cups (2 L) chicken broth
½ cup (125 mL) grated
 Parmesan cheese
Salt and freshly ground pepper

Heat half the oil in a medium skillet. Remove the sausage meat from the casing and add it to the skillet along with the chopped onion. Cook, breaking up the meat, until the onions are browned and the meat is cooked through. Add the minced garlic and cook for an additional minute. Set aside while the risotto is cooking.

Place the broth in a saucepan and heat over low heat. Heat the remaining oil over medium heat in a large heavy pot. Add the rice to the oil and stir to coat. Add the wine and stir with a wooden spoon until it is absorbed. Begin adding the warm broth about 1 cup (250 mL) at a time. Continue to stir the risotto while the broth is absorbing. When it is fully absorbed, add another cup of broth. Continue this process until all the broth is used up.

Add the cooked sausage and Parmesan cheese. Stir and heat through. Add pepper and salt if needed. Serve immediately.

Beef Satay with Peanut Sauce

Serves 6 to 8

The kids love this dish and they always request it for spring or summer birthday barbecues. It is made with flank steak. Soaking the bamboo skewers in water prevents them from burning on the grills. The meat should marinate for several hours, so start preparing this dish in the afternoon. Serve Lemon Potatoes and Asian Cabbage Salad as accompaniment.

If you don't want to bother slicing the steak and threading it on skewers, simply place the whole steaks in the marinade for several hours or overnight. After barbecuing the meat, let it sit for 10 minutes before slicing. Serve with the peanut sauce.

2 to 3 flank steaks
20 to 25 – 10- or 12-inch (25 to 30 cm)
　bamboo skewers

MARINADE

2 cloves garlic, mashed
¼ cup (60 mL) chopped cilantro
3 tablespoons (45 mL) brown sugar
2 teaspoons (10 mL) ground coriander
⅓ cup (75 mL) soy sauce
¼ cup (60 mL) lime juice
4 tablespoons (60 mL) sunflower oil

PEANUT SAUCE

1 clove garlic, mashed
1–2 tablespoons (15–30 mL) chopped
　fresh ginger
1 green onion, white part only
2 slices pickled jalapeño peppers
¼ cup (60 mL) peanut butter
3 tablespoons (45 mL) coconut milk
　or buttermilk
2 sprigs cilantro or parsley
2 teaspoons (10 mL) soy sauce
1 tablespoon (15 mL) lime juice
1½ teaspoons (7 mL) brown sugar
Freshly ground pepper

Soak the bamboo skewers in warm water for at least 10 minutes. Combine marinade ingredients in a bowl big enough to hold the meat and set aside. Slice the flank steak diagonally, across the grain, into about ¼ inch (.5 cm) slices. They will be long and thin. Place the meat in the marinade and refrigerate for 1 to 4 hours.

Dry the skewers. Begin skewering the meat by threading it over and under along the length of the strips of meat. You may put 2 slices of meat on each skewer depending on the original size of the flank. Set the skewers on a plate as you go.

Combine all of the peanut sauce ingredients in the bowl of a food processor or use a handheld blender. Pulse mixture until well combined. Pour into small serving dish.

Preheat the barbecue to medium-high. The skewers will not take long to barbecue so you will need to keep your eye on them. Turn them over after 3 to 4 minutes. You can keep the cooked ones warm in a low oven while the others are on the barbecue.

Serve skewers with the peanut sauce passed in a small bowl.

Make a double batch of this peanut sauce for a pasta salad.

Rack of Lamb with Rosemary, Garlic and Dijon

Serves 6 to 8

This is an easy dish to prepare for family and guests. You can have the lamb all prepared with the Dijon paste early in the day and put in the oven just before dinner. When timing your meal, be sure to add on the 10 minutes the racks need to sit when they come out of the oven.

3 racks (600 grams each) of lamb
3 tablespoons (45 mL) chopped fresh rosemary
2 cloves garlic, mashed
1 teaspoon (5 mL) salt
½ cup (125 mL) Dijon mustard
1 tablespoon (15 mL) balsamic vinegar

Preheat oven to 450F (230C). Line a baking sheet with foil. Lay the 3 racks out on the baking sheet with the bones curved down.

Combine rosemary, garlic, salt, Dijon and balsamic vinegar in a small bowl and stir well.

Spread one-third of the paste over the top of each rack. Bake in preheated oven 20 minutes for rare, 25 minutes for medium. Remove from oven, cover with foil and let sit 10 minutes.

Serve with Lemon Potatoes and a tossed green salad.

Beef Tenderloin with Dijon Rub   Serves 12

Tenderloin is an expensive cut of meat, but it is so easy to prepare when you are feeding a crowd. The marinade can be rubbed on the meat early in the day. The beef can be cooked in a hot oven or on the barbecue.

1 – 5- to 6-pound (2.5 to 3 kg) beef tenderloin

RUB
⅓ cup (75 mL) Dijon mustard
2 tablespoons (30 mL) soy sauce
3 large garlic cloves, mashed
4 teaspoons (20 mL) chopped fresh rosemary
½ teaspoon (2 mL) freshly ground pepper
2 tablespoons (30 mL) olive oil

Combine the rub ingredients. Trim any excess fat from the meat. Cover the meat with the rub. This can be done up to 1 hour ahead of cooking and left out at room temperature. If you prepare the meat earlier in the day, keep it refrigerated until about 30 minutes before cooking.

Preheat oven to 400F (200C). Set the meat in a roasting pan and cook in preheated oven until a meat thermometer measures 120 to 125F (50 to 52C) for rare to medium-rare meat, 60 to 75 minutes.

For barbecued beef, preheat the grills on high heat. Turn off the centre element and cook the meat over indirect heat until the internal temperature measures 120 to 125F (50 to 52C). It will take about 60 to 75 minutes.

Let the meat sit for about 10 minutes before slicing. Serve with Mushroom Madeira Gravy or Beef Gravy.

A MEAT THERMOMETER PROBE is an invaluable tool for cooking a cut of meat and is well worth the investment. The probe stays in the meat during cooking and the temperature of the meat can be read outside the oven or barbecue. It will cost you less than the piece of meat!

Beef Gravy

Makes about 4 cups (1 L)

It is not always possible to make gravy from pan drippings. When you are barbecuing a roast, or if you want a sauce to go with a steak, you can make this gravy ahead of time and reheat it before serving. Cooking the vegetables until they are nice and brown is the trick here: it adds both colour and flavour.

3 tablespoons (45 mL) butter
1 medium onion, coarsely chopped
2 carrots, coarsely chopped
2 stalks celery, coarsely chopped
2 cloves garlic, coarsely chopped
2 bay leaves
1 sprig rosemary
3 tablespoons (45 mL) flour
2 tablespoons (30 mL) tomato paste
4 cups (1 L) beef broth
¼ cup (60 mL) red wine
1 tablespoon (15 mL) balsamic vinegar
1 teaspoon (5 mL) browning and seasoning sauce
Salt and freshly ground pepper

Brown the carrots, celery, onion, garlic, bay leaf and rosemary in the butter over medium high heat for 10 to 15 minutes. When they are becoming brown and starting to stick to the bottom of the pan, add the flour and cook 1 to 2 minutes. Add the tomato paste and the broth. Bring to a boil; add the wine, vinegar and seasoning sauce. Continue to boil the sauce until it reduces a bit.

Strain the sauce through a sieve set over a bowl, pushing through some of the solids, and return the sauce to the pan. Continue to reduce and thicken if required. Add any pan juices that you may have. Taste for seasoning.

This gravy can be made ahead and frozen.

Mushroom Madeira Gravy

Makes about 3 cups (750 mL)

I like to do as much as I can ahead of time, especially when we are having guests. This gravy can go with any meat but is extra good with Beef Tenderloin. If I barbecue the beef, I don't get the drippings to make a sauce, so this gravy works well.

2 tablespoons (30 mL) olive oil
1 tablespoon (15 mL) butter
½ cup (125 mL) chopped shallots
2 cups (500 mL) coarsely chopped mushrooms
2 cloves garlic, mashed
½ cup (125 mL) Madeira wine
3 tablespoons (45 mL) tomato paste
1 teaspoon (5 mL) chopped fresh rosemary
2 cups (500 mL) beef broth plus ¼ cup (60 mL)
    beef broth
1 tablespoon (15 mL) cornstarch

Heat the butter and olive oil together in a medium saucepan. Add the shallots and mushrooms and cook, stirring frequently, over medium-high heat until the liquid from the mushrooms is absorbed and they are nice and brown. Add the garlic and let it cook with the mushroom mixture for about 30 seconds. Deglaze the pan by adding the Madeira, scraping up the bottom of the pan. Let it boil for about a minute.

Add the 2 cups (500 mL) beef broth, tomato paste and rosemary. Bring the gravy to a boil and let it simmer for about 5 minutes. In a small cup combine the remaining ¼ cup (60 mL) broth with the cornstarch. Add this mixture to the sauce and stir for 1 or 2 minutes until the sauce is thickened.

If you are making this sauce ahead of time, transfer it to a smaller saucepan with a lid and refrigerate. It can be made 1 or 2 days ahead. Warm before serving. This gravy can also be frozen.

Grilled Boneless Leg of Lamb with Dijon Mustard Marinade

Serves 8 to 10

This lamb dish is so easy to prepare. You can make up the marinade and put the lamb and marinade into a re-sealable bag 1 or 2 days ahead of time. It is perfect to take away for the weekend as it can all be prepared in advance.

1 – 3- to 3½-pound (1.5 to 2 kg) boneless
   leg of lamb

DIJON MARINADE

3 garlic cloves, mashed
½ cup (125 mL) Dijon mustard
1 teaspoon (5 mL) salt
3 tablespoons (45 mL) lemon juice
2 tablespoons (30 mL) chopped fresh rosemary
¼ cup (60 mL) olive oil
½ teaspoon (2 mL) freshly ground pepper

SPICED RED CURRANTS are an excellent condiment to serve with lamb (see recipe on page 180).

Combine the marinade ingredients in a small bowl. Trim the lamb of any excess fat or gristle. Place the lamb in a large re-sealable bag. Pour marinade over lamb and seal the bag, eliminating as much air as possible. Refrigerate the lamb for up to 48 hours.

Remove the lamb from the fridge about 1 hour before grilling. Preheat the barbecue to high heat. Lay the lamb, skin side down, on the hot grill. Close the barbecue lid and allow the meat to sear for 4 to 5 minutes. Turn the lamb over and sear the other side for another 4 to 5 minutes. Turn off the middle element of the barbecue and cook the lamb over indirect heat for an additional 30 to 45 minutes depending on the thickness. The internal temperature of a meat thermometer should read 125 to 130F (55C). Remove the lamb from the barbecue and let sit for an additional 10 minutes before slicing.

Lamb Stew

Serves 8 to 10

This lamb stew can be made one or two days ahead, which makes it a wonderful dish for entertaining. It also freezes very well.

4 to 5 pound (2 to 2.5 kg) boneless lamb leg
Salt and freshly ground pepper
4 tablespoons (60 mL) vegetable oil
1 tablespoon (15 mL) sugar
6 tablespoons (90 mL) flour
4 cups (1 L) beef broth
1½ cups (325 mL) tomato sauce
1 tablespoon (15 mL) chopped fresh rosemary
2 tablespoons (30 mL) tomato paste

2 large garlic cloves, mashed
1 large Russet potato, peeled and cut into ¾-inch (1.5 cm) dice
2 to 3 carrots, peeled and cut into ¾-inch (1.5 cm) dice
1 small turnip, peeled and cut into ¾-inch (1.5 cm) dice

1 cup (250 mL) frozen peas

Preheat oven to 450F (230C).

Trim the fat from the lamb and cut it into 1½ inch (3 cm) cubes. Place in a bowl lined with paper towel to absorb any juices. Sprinkle the meat with ½ teaspoon (2 mL) each of salt and pepper. In a large skillet heat about 2 tablespoons (30 mL) oil over medium high heat.

Brown the meat in batches on all sides. Transfer to a large heavy oven-proof pot with a tight-fitting lid. Continue until all of the meat is browned. Sprinkle the meat with sugar and place in preheated oven, uncovered, to caramelize the sugar. This will take about 5 to 7 minutes, stirring once or twice. Remove the pot from the oven and stir in the flour. Return the pot to the oven to cook the flour. This will take 4 to 5 minutes.

Turn oven heat down to 350F (180C). Remove pot from the oven and stir in the broth, tomato sauce, rosemary, tomato paste and garlic. Bring the mixture to a boil over medium heat and check for seasoning. Cover the pot and return to oven for 30 minutes. After 30 minutes, add the potatoes, carrots and turnips, stirring to coat with sauce. Return the stew to the oven for 1 hour more. Remove from oven and stir in the frozen peas. Cool and refrigerate if serving later. Reheat the stew at 325F (160C) for about 1 hour before serving.

Five-Hour Beef Stew

Serves 6

You don't have to brown the meat for this easy beef stew. Just combine all the ingredients in the pot and put it in the oven for five hours without peeking. If you would like to make it a day ahead, cook it for four hours the first day and reheat it for 1 hour the day you serve it. The sauce is thick and tasty. The tapioca dissolves as the stew cooks.

3 cups (750 mL) vegetable or tomato juice
1½ tablespoons (22 mL) Dijon mustard
2 tablespoons (30 mL) brown sugar
¼ cup (60 mL) small pearl tapioca
2 cloves garlic, mashed
1 teaspoon (5 mL) dried oregano
1 bay leaf
1 teaspoon (5 mL) salt
½ teaspoon (2 mL) freshly ground pepper

2½ pounds (1.5 kg) beef stew meat, cut in
    1½-inch (3 cm) pieces
3 carrots, peeled and cut into 1 x ½-inch
    (2 x 1 cm) sticks
3 stalks celery, peeled and cut in ½-inch
    (1 cm) pieces
2 large Russet potatoes, peeled and
    cut in ¾-inch (1.5 cm) chunks
1 medium onion, diced

Preheat oven to 275F (135C). Use a heavy ovenproof pot with a tight-fitting lid. Place vegetable or tomato juice, Dijon mustard, brown sugar, tapioca, garlic, oregano, bay leaf, salt and pepper in the pot. Stir well. Add the beef, carrots, celery, potato and onions. Stir everything together. Place lid on pot. Put in oven and don't peek or touch for the full five hours. Remove bay leaf. Serve with fresh bread and tossed green salad.

Many of my recipes call for dried herbs because they are always available. I do have a herb garden right outside my kitchen and I have bay leaves and rosemary most of the year. If using fresh herbs, the general rule of thumb is to double the amount given for dried herbs. For example, if a recipe calls for 1 teaspoon of dried oregano, use 2 teaspoons of fresh, chopped.

Meatballs with Barbecue Sauce

Serves 6

If you prefer, use purchased frozen meatballs instead of making them. Bake them in the oven before adding them to the sauce. Instead of Rice Pilaf, serve the meatballs with plain rice. I like to combine half white and half brown rice (try some basmati rice).

BARBECUE SAUCE

1 medium onion, finely chopped
2 garlic cloves, mashed
1 tablespoon (15 mL) butter
1 tablespoon (15 mL) oil
1½ cups (325 mL) chicken broth
2¾ cups (700 mL) tomato sauce
¾ cup (175 mL) tomato ketchup
1 tablespoon (15 mL) Dijon mustard

1 teaspoon (5 mL) Worcestershire sauce
3 tablespoons (45 mL) brown sugar
2 tablespoons (30 mL) lemon juice
Salt and freshly ground pepper
¼ teaspoon (1 mL) hot sauce
2 tablespoons (30 mL) sweet
   Thai chili sauce
2 tablespoons (30 mL) tomato paste

Melt butter and oil. Add onion and cook until soft. Add garlic; cook 1 more minute. Add broth, tomato sauce, ketchup, mustard, Worcestershire sauce, brown sugar, lemon juice, salt, pepper, hot sauce, chili sauce and tomato paste. Bring to simmer and cook 10 to 15 minutes.

MEATBALLS

2 pounds (1 kg) lean ground beef
½ cup (125 mL) finely minced onion
1 cup (250 mL) panko (Japanese
   breadcrumbs) or ¾ cup (175 mL)
   regular dried breadcrumbs
1 tablespoon (15 mL) Dijon mustard
1 egg
Pinch of cayenne
1 teaspoon (5 mL) dried oregano
½ teaspoon (2 mL) salt
Freshly ground pepper

Combine all meatball ingredients. Form into small balls. Brown the meatballs in a skillet in 2 tablespoons (30 mL) oil. Add to barbecue sauce. Heat everything together over low heat 30 to 45 minutes, or heat in oven at 350F (180C) for 45 minutes.

RICE PILAF

¼ cup (60 mL) butter
½ cup (125 mL) finely chopped onion
2 cups (500 mL) rice
4¼ cups (1L plus 60 mL) chicken stock
2 tablespoons (30 mL) chopped fresh parsley

Melt butter in medium heavy pot with tight-fitting lid. Cook onion until soft. Add rice and cook several minutes. Add stock, bring to boil. Put lid on pot and place in a 350F (180C) oven for 45 minutes. Add parsley and fluff with a fork.

Pork Tenderloin with Asian Marinade

Serves 6 to 8

The pork can be marinated for a couple of hours or up to a day ahead.
You can serve it with the Peanut Sauce recipe in Beef Satay (see page 72).

2 to 3 pork tenderloins

½ cup (125 mL) sunflower oil
¼ cup (60 mL) soy sauce

3 to 4 cloves garlic, mashed
¼ cup (60 mL) chopped fresh ginger
¼ cup (60 mL) chopped parsley

For the marinade, combine all the ingredients in a small bowl. Place the pork tenderloins in a large re-sealable bag and pour marinade into the bag. Seal the bag, removing as much of the air as possible. If you prefer, you can set the meat in a glass pan and pour the marinade over top. If you use this method, be sure to turn the pork several times as it marinates.

Heat the barbecue to high. Remove the pork from the marinade, letting any excess drip off. Place the pork on the barbecue to sear for 4 to 5 minutes on each side. Turn the barbecue down to medium and cook the pork until it is no longer pink in the centre.

Let the meat sit for several minutes on a cutting board before slicing.

Beef Short Ribs with Rub and Barbecue Sauce

Serves 6 to 8

I use my slow cooker for these ribs, but it is fine to make them in a heavy pot with a tight-fitting lid and cook them in the oven. It's best to begin cooking the ribs the day before, because the next day it will be easy to remove the solidified fat after they have been in the fridge overnight. If you don't have time to make a barbecue sauce, use bottled sauce. You will need about 2½ to 3 cups.

3 to 4 pounds (1.5 to 2 kg) thick-cut short ribs (about 12 ribs)
2 to 3 tablespoons (30 to 45 mL) oil

RUB FOR RIBS

2 teaspoons (10 mL) salt
1 teaspoon (5 mL) freshly ground pepper
2 tablespoons (30 mL) brown sugar
1 teaspoon (5 mL) paprika
1 teaspoon (5 mL) dried thyme or oregano

1 teaspoon (5 mL) chili powder
1 teaspoon (5 mL) cumin
½ teaspoon (2 mL) mustard powder
½ teaspoon (2 mL) celery seed
¼ teaspoon (1 mL) cayenne pepper

Combine rub ingredients, using this recipe as a guide. You can add whatever spices you like once you have the salt and sugar proportions. Put the rub in a shallow dish. Coat each rib with rub. In a large heavy pot, heat oil over medium high heat. Brown the ribs on all sides in batches. Place in slow cooker dish or heavy ovenproof dish.

BARBECUE SAUCE

1 medium onion, finely diced
1 tablespoon (15 mL) olive oil
1 clove garlic, mashed
1½ cups (325 mL) chili sauce or tomato sauce
2 tablespoons (30 mL) molasses
2 tablespoons (30 mL) Dijon mustard

2 tablespoons (30 mL) red or
  white wine vinegar
2 tablespoons (30 mL) brown sugar
1 tablespoon (15 mL) Worcestershire
  sauce
½ teaspoon (2 mL) freshly ground pepper
¼ cup (60 mL) water

Make barbecue sauce in the same pot used for the ribs. It may be necessary to rinse it out if the bottom is very black. Sauté chopped onion in oil over medium heat about 5 minutes, until soft but not brown. Add garlic, sauté 1 minute more. Add chili sauce or tomato sauce, molasses, Dijon mustard, vinegar, brown sugar, Worcestershire, pepper and water. Simmer the sauce for about 10 minutes. Pour sauce over short ribs and turn on slow cooker set for 4 to 5 hours on high. If cooking ribs in the oven, return the ribs to the sauce, cover with lid and cook in 350F (180C) oven for 1½ hours.

Refrigerate the ribs overnight and remove any hardened fat before reheating them in the slow cooker for about 2 hours on high or 4 to 6 hours on low, or in a 350F (180C) oven for about 1 hour.

Serve the short ribs with rice, mashed potatoes or pasta. This is a great dinner to come home to after a long afternoon of activities.

Steak with Peppercorn Sauce
Serves 6

Serve this steak with Seasoned Potato Wedges (see page 52) and you will feel as if you're in Paris eating "steak and frites."

This is a quick and easy sauce to serve with any steak. This recipe calls for a pan-fried steak. After the steak is fried and set aside, the sauce is returned to the pan to collect any more juices and flavour. Pass extra sauce at the table. You could also broil or barbecue the steak.

PEPPERCORN SAUCE

2 tablespoons (30 mL) butter
2 large shallots, finely chopped
1 teaspoon (5 mL) drained green
  peppercorns in brine
2 cups (500 mL) beef broth

½ cup (125 mL) brandy
¼ cup (60 mL) whipping cream

2 tablespoons (30 mL) olive oil
2 pounds (1 kg) top sirloin steak
  (about 1-inch/2 cm thick)

Melt 1 tablespoon (15 mL) butter in heavy medium saucepan over medium-high heat. Add shallots and sauté until beginning to brown, about 5 minutes. Add peppercorns and mash with the back of a fork. Add broth, brandy and cream and boil until sauce is thick enough to coat spoon, whisking occasionally, about 15 minutes. Set sauce aside in a bowl.

Melt remaining 1 tablespoon (15 mL) butter with olive oil in heavy large skillet over medium-high heat. Sprinkle steak with salt and pepper. Add steak to skillet and sauté until brown and cooked to desired doneness, about 5 minutes per side for medium-rare. Transfer steak to cutting board. Add reserved sauce to same skillet and heat, stirring to scrape up browned bits.

Slice the steak and serve it on a plate with a small amount of sauce.

Barbecued Tri-Tip Steaks

Serves 10 to 12

The cut of beef called for here may not be readily available. You may have to ask the butcher to cut it for you. It is almost like a thick flank steak that you slice thinly before serving. If you can't find this particular cut, try using a sirloin steak at least 1 inch (2 cm) thick.

Gordon loves his meat and potatoes. For his birthday dinner I prepared this steak, along with some Spiced Roasted Potatoes, Greek Salad and Asian Cabbage Salad. I also served Roasted Asparagus and bread.

2 to 2½-pounds (1.25 kg) tri-tip, sirloin or flatiron steaks

SPICE RUB

¼ cup (60 mL) packed brown sugar
1 tablespoon (15 mL) ground cumin
1 tablespoon (15 mL) chili powder
2 teaspoons (10 mL) salt
1 teaspoon (5 mL) freshly ground pepper
1 teaspoon (5 mL) mustard powder

BARBECUE SAUCE

1 large onion, finely chopped
2 tablespoons (30 mL) olive oil
1 cup ketchup or chili sauce
3 tablespoons (45 mL)
  Worcestershire sauce
¼ cup (60 mL) water

Combine the ingredients for the spice rub. Pat the steaks dry with paper towel. Rub the steaks all over with 3 to 4 tablespoons (45 to 60 mL) of the spice rub. This can be done earlier in the day. Set them in a glass pan, cover and refrigerate until about 1 hour before barbecuing. If you don't have time, you can cover them in the rub and let them sit out at room temperature for about 1 hour.

In a heavy saucepan, sauté the onion in the oil over medium heat for 5 to 7 minutes until it starts to become golden brown. Add the ketchup or chili sauce, Worcestershire sauce and remaining spices from the rub. Bring to boil, turn down heat and simmer about 10 minutes. Add the water and purée the sauce in a blender, or with a handheld blender. It should be nice and smooth. Set about ¼ cup (60 mL) barbecue sauce aside and put the rest in a bowl to serve at the table.

Preheat the barbecue on high heat for about 10 minutes. When it is hot, place the steaks on the barbecue, close the lid and cook them over high heat for 4 to 5 minutes. Turn them over and cook an additional 4 to 5 minutes with the lid closed. Brush the steaks on both sides with the reserved barbecue sauce.

Turn the heat down to medium and continue to cook the steaks until the interior temperature measures about 120 to 125F (50 to 52C). It will only take another 10 to 15 minutes or so, depending on the thickness of the meat. This will give you a good mix of medium and rare meat.

Remove the steaks from the barbecue and let them sit for about 10 minutes before slicing. Serve the steaks with the additional barbecue sauce at the table.

Beef Lettuce Wrap

Serves 6

This is all you need for a complete meal. It is easy and fun to eat.

FILLING

2 pounds (1 kg) lean ground beef
½ cup (125 mL) chopped onion
1 red pepper, diced
1 green pepper, diced
2 carrots, peeled and grated
1 – 8-ounce (250 mL) can water
   chestnuts, chopped
1 clove garlic, mashed
4 green onions, chopped

ASIAN SAUCE

1½ cups (325 mL) hoisin sauce
1 tablespoon (15 mL) rice vinegar
2 tablespoons (30 mL) liquid honey
2 tablespoons (30 mL) fresh lime juice
1 tablespoon (15 mL) sesame oil
1 clove garlic, mashed
2 teaspoons (10 mL) fresh grated ginger

1 large or 2 small heads iceberg lettuce

In a large skillet brown the meat with the chopped onion. When the meat is no longer pink, drain any accumulated fat and then add the peppers. Cook 1 minute. Add the carrots, water chestnuts, garlic and green onions; cook 1 to 2 more minutes.

Mix sauce ingredients together in a microwave-proof dish and heat on high 2 to 3 minutes, or heat in a small saucepan on the stove. Stir enough sauce into meat to coat lightly, ½ to ¾ cup (125 to 175 mL).

Core lettuces, slice in half and separate leaves. Wash well and pile in a bowl. Place the meat mixture in a serving dish. Put the sauce in a small bowl with a serving spoon. Everybody can help themselves at the table to put as much meat as they like on a lettuce leaf, with sauce to their taste, then rolling up the wrap.

Substitute ground turkey or chicken if you prefer.

Roast Beef and Yorkshire Pudding with Roast Potatoes and Gravy

Serves 8 to 10

When I was growing up we had a roast of some kind for dinner every Sunday. There were usually leftovers on Monday night. These days we often invite our "grannies" for dinner on Sunday nights for Roast Beef and Yorkshire Pudding. You don't need to spend all day in the kitchen; this recipe will help you get the timing down.

A bone-in prime rib, although quite expensive, is a beautiful marbled cut of meat and tastes so good. If you prefer, you can use a baron of beef. A baron of beef will not have a bone, so it will go further and you will have more leftovers. Ask the butcher to give you an extra piece of fat for making gravy.

1 – 5- to 6-pound (2½ to 3 kg) beef roast
3 tablespoons (45 mL) Dijon mustard
Salt and freshly ground pepper
Extra fat

YORKSHIRE PUDDING

3 eggs
1½ cups (375 mL) whole milk or
    1 cup (250 mL) low-fat milk + ½ cup
    (125 mL) light cream
1½ teaspoons (7 mL) salt
1⅓ cups (330 mL) flour

½ cup (125 mL) butter, clarified
Olive oil
Beef fat, if there is enough

ROAST POTATOES

6 Russet potatoes
3 tablespoons (45 mL) olive oil
Salt and freshly ground pepper

GRAVY

Flour (about ½ cup/125 mL)
Beef broth (about 4 cups/1L)
Cooking liquid from vegetables
    (about 2 cups/500 mL)
1 teaspoon (5 mL) browning and
    seasoning sauce
Salt and freshly ground pepper

Take the roast out of the fridge about 1 hour before you begin cooking it.

Preheat oven to 350F (180C). Turn on convection if you have it. Spread the Dijon mustard over the top of the beef. Sprinkle generously with salt and pepper. Place in a roasting pan, preferably on a rack. Using a rack is particularly important with a convection oven as it lets the air circulate around the meat. Lay extra fat on top of the roast and put the pan in the oven.

For the Yorkshire Pudding, combine the eggs, milk, salt and flour and blend well with an electric mixer or a handheld blender. Let the mixture sit out at room temperature for 1 to 3 hours.

I make my puddings in muffin tins. This recipe makes 18 of them. Each muffin tin needs about 2 teaspoons (10 mL) of fat. I rarely have enough beef fat so I use a mixture of ¼ cup (60 mL) olive oil and ⅓ cup (80 mL) clarified butter. Divide this butter and oil mixture between the 18 muffin cups.

Peel the potatoes and quarter lengthwise. Toss with olive oil and salt and pepper. Place on a baking sheet and roast them in the oven with the meat. They will take about 45 minutes to 1 hour to roast. Stir them from time to time so that they brown evenly. When they are cooked, transfer to a serving bowl and cover to keep warm, or place in a warming oven.

A 2½ kg roast will take about 1¾ to 2 hours to cook in a convection oven. In a regular oven it will take 2 to 2½ hours. I use a meat thermometer and take the roast out of the oven when the internal temperature reads about 120F (50C). This gives a medium-rare roast.

The roast should sit on the carving board covered with foil and then a tea towel for at least 20 minutes. Discard the large pieces of fat. The cutting board should have a well around the outside to catch any juices. The juices will be added to the gravy.

CLARIFIED BUTTER — Melt about ½ cup (125 mL) butter in the microwave or in a small saucepan. Skim the foam off the top and pour the butter into another container, leaving behind any solids in the bottom of the first container. Clarified butter can tolerate high temperatures without burning. After the butter is clarified you will have about ⅓ cup (80 mL).

When the roast is removed from the oven turn the temperature up to 425F (220C) for the Yorkshire Puddings.

Meanwhile begin making the gravy. Place the roasting pan with the liquid fat in it on the stove and turn on 1 or 2 elements to medium low. Slowly begin adding some flour, whisking constantly. If you have about ½ cup (125 mL) of fat in the pan, you will need an equal amount of flour. If you don't have that much fat add some butter to make up the difference. The flour and fat mixture should be a smooth paste and not too lumpy. Cook the flour for several minutes. Add about 6 cups of broth and vegetable juices combined. Bring the gravy to a boil, stirring frequently as it thickens. Turn down to simmer. Add the browning and seasoning sauce and salt and pepper to taste. Add any juices from the carving board. Adjust the liquid, adding more if needed to thin down the gravy. Just before serving, transfer to a gravy boat or a jug to pass at the table.

For the Yorkshire Puddings: when the oven temperature is up to 425F (220C), place the muffin tins with the butter and oil in them in the oven for 1 to 2 minutes. Don't forget about them! Remove from the oven and quickly divide the Yorkshire Pudding batter among the 18 cups. Quickly return to the oven and set the timer for 15 minutes. The puddings should rise up in the muffin cups; check them after 15 minutes and turn the temperature down to 400F (200C). They may need 5 or 10 more minutes. You will want to serve dinner as soon as they are ready. Begin carving the beef when the puddings are in the oven.

fish & seafood

Most seafood dishes make a quick and easy weeknight meal for families. For some children, seafood can be a "hard sell." Just ask them to try a bite each time you serve it and eventually they will probably come to like it. Buy fish that is really fresh.

Fish Baked in Tomato and Bacon Sauce

Serves 6

Here is a quick and easy weeknight meal with just a bit of bacon for added flavour. Use any kind of fresh white fish.

2 to 2½ pounds (1 to 1.5 kg) white fish
　　such as cod or snapper
5 to 6 slices bacon
1 medium onion, chopped
1 clove garlic, mashed
½ cup (125 mL) white wine
1½ cups (375 mL) fresh tomatoes, diced
1 tablespoon (15 mL) capers, chopped
Salt and freshly ground pepper

Preheat oven to 400F (200C). Slice the bacon crosswise into thin strips and fry in a medium skillet until crisp. Drain on paper towel. Pour off all but 1 tablespoon (15 mL) bacon fat, reserving the remainder in a small bowl.

Lightly season the fish with salt and pepper. Heat the 1 tablespoon (15 mL) bacon fat to medium high heat. Brown the fish for about 1 to 2 minutes per side. Transfer to an oven-proof dish.

Heat another 1 tablespoon (15 mL) bacon fat in a skillet. Add chopped onion and cook until soft and beginning to brown. Add the garlic, cook another minute or so. Add the wine and boil to reduce by half, less than a minute. Add the tomatoes, bacon and the capers. Season with salt and pepper. Cook 3 to 5 minutes. Pour over fish and bake 25 to 30 minutes until the fish is firm to the touch.

When I am serving fish to children (and adults), I am very careful to remove all the bones. A bad experience with fish bones could last a lifetime. Good tweezers kept in your kitchen drawer work very well for this. Run your finger along the flesh of the fish to feel the bones and pull them out.

Halibut with Tomato and Avocado Salsa

Serves 6

Halibut is such a mild fish even non-fish eaters might like it. The salsa is very tasty and would work well over any fish. Serve this dish with a fresh salad and some rice for a quick and easy dinner.

MARINADE FOR FISH

2 pounds (1 kg) halibut fillets
2 tablespoons (30 mL) olive oil
Juice of 1 lime
¼ teaspoon (1 mL) hot sauce

TOMATO AND AVOCADO SALSA

1 large or 2 medium tomatoes
1 ripe but firm avocado, diced

2 tablespoons (30 mL) white wine vinegar
¼ cup (60 mL) sliced green onions
2 to 3 slices pickled jalapeños, chopped
2 to 3 tablespoons (30 to 45 mL) chopped
   cilantro or flat leaf parsley
2 tablespoons (30 mL) olive oil
½ teaspoon (2 mL) salt
¼ teaspoon (1 mL) freshly ground pepper

Cut halibut into 6 serving-size pieces. Set them in a glass or ceramic baking dish. Pour olive oil, lime juice and hot sauce over top. Cover and refrigerate for 1 to 4 hours.

To make the salsa, core the tomatoes and cut them in half. With your fingers, remove some of the seeds and juice. Dice the tomato in ½ inch (1 cm) cubes. Place them in a bowl and add diced avocado, vinegar, green onions, jalapeños, cilantro, oil and salt and pepper. Stir lightly to combine. This can be made several hours in advance. Cover well and refrigerate.

Preheat oven to 400F (200C). Bake halibut for about 25 minutes or until firm to the touch. You can cook it on the barbecue, on a piece of foil, if you prefer. Pass the salsa at the table.

Salmon Fillet with Maple & Soy

Serves 6

2 to 2½-pounds (1 to 1.5 kg) salmon fillets

MARINADE

1 clove garlic, mashed
1 teaspoon (5 mL) fresh ginger, grated
   or chopped

3 tablespoons (45 mL) maple syrup
2 tablespoons (30 mL) soy sauce
½ teaspoon (2 mL) sesame oil

If you are using the small food processor to make the marinade, you don't have to mash the garlic or chop the ginger. Place them both in the processor and chop them up before you add the maple syrup, soy sauce and sesame oil. Pour the marinade into a shallow ovenproof dish big enough to hold the piece of salmon. Lay the salmon flesh side down over the marinade. Cover and chill, preferably for 1 hour but at least for 10 minutes.

Preheat oven to 400F (200C). Flip the salmon over so that it is skin side down. Bake in preheated oven about 20 minutes. You can tell if the salmon is done by touching it with your finger at the fattest part. It should feel firm to the touch. If not, give it a few more minutes.

Serve salmon with stir-fry veggies and rice.

Salmon with Curry Mayonnaise Serves 6

2 pounds (1 kg) salmon fillet, skin on,
    bones removed
2 tablespoons (30 mL) butter
1 clove garlic, mashed

¼ teaspoon (1 mL) salt
Freshly ground pepper
¾ cup (175 mL) mayonnaise
1 teaspoon (5 mL) curry powder

Preheat oven to 375F (190C).

Melt the butter and add the garlic, salt and pepper. Cool to room temperature. Lay the salmon fillet, skin side down, onto a foil-lined baking sheet. Spread butter mixture on top. Bake the fish in the preheated oven for 20 to 25 minutes, or until the flesh is firm to the touch at the thickest point. The salmon can also be cooked on the barbecue over medium-high heat, on foil.

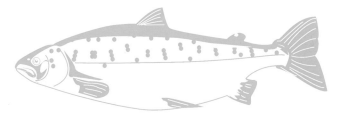

While the fish is cooking, combine mayonnaise and curry powder. Place in small serving dish.

When salmon is cooked, cut into serving pieces and pass the sauce at the table.

Baked Seafood with Tomato Sauce and Feta Cheese

Serves 8

This dish is just delicious. You can make it ahead of time so it is perfect for entertaining. Good quality frozen fish works well if you can't get fresh. Use any combination of fish, depending on your taste, or what is available.

TOMATO SAUCE

2 tablespoons (30 mL) olive oil
1 medium onion, finely chopped
1 clove garlic, mashed
1 bay leaf
1 teaspoon (5 mL) sugar
¼ cup (60 mL) dry white wine
1 – 28-ounce (796 mL) can whole or
    diced tomatoes
2 tablespoons (30 mL) fresh chopped parsley
½ teaspoon (2 mL) salt
¼ teaspoon (1 mL) freshly ground pepper

FISH AND SEAFOOD

1 pound (500 grams) large shrimp or
    prawns, peeled
1½ pounds (750 grams) halibut or other
    white fish, skinned, boned and cut into
    1½ inch (3 cm) pieces
½ pound (250 grams) feta cheese
½ cup (125 mL) dry breadcrumbs or
    panko (Japanese bread crumbs)
3 tablespoons (45 mL) melted butter
3 tablespoons (45 mL) chopped parsley

To make the tomato sauce, heat the oil in a medium saucepan and cook the onion until soft but not brown, 3 to 5 minutes. Add the garlic, cook an additional minute. If you are using canned whole tomatoes, chop them with a handheld blender before adding them to the sauce. Add bay leaf, sugar, wine and tomatoes to the onions. Bring sauce to boil, reduce heat and simmer 20 to 30 minutes. Add the 2 tablespoons (30 mL) parsley, salt and pepper. Turn off heat and cool sauce before pouring it over the seafood.

Preheat oven to 375F (190C). Butter a 13 x 9 x 2-inch (3.5 L) glass or ceramic baking dish. Sprinkle the feta cheese over the bottom of the dish. Lay fish and seafood over the cheese in a single layer. Pour tomato sauce on top. Combine breadcrumbs with melted butter and remaining 3 tablespoons (45 mL) chopped parsley. Sprinkle on top of casserole. If making ahead, cover well and refrigerate.

Bake the casserole for about 45 minutes until hot and bubbly around the edges.

Linguine with Clam Sauce

Serves 6

Some nights you just don't know what to make for dinner and there is no time to go to the store. You will most likely have all of the ingredients for this recipe on hand. It's quick and easy. Salad and French bread are all you need to complete this meal.

2 tablespoons (30 mL) butter
1 large onion, chopped
2 cloves garlic, mashed
¾ cup (175 mL) white wine
2 – 10-ounce (142 gram) cans baby clams

2 to 3 tablespoons (30 to 45 mL)
   chopped parsley
Salt and freshly ground pepper

1 pound (500 grams) linguine or other pasta
Parmesan cheese for serving

Bring a large pot of salted water to a boil for the pasta. Meanwhile melt the butter in a medium skillet and cook the chopped onion for about 5 minutes over medium heat. Add the garlic and cook, stirring, for another minute. Add the wine, clams with juice and parsley; season with salt and pepper. Simmer about 5 minutes.

When the pasta is cooked, drain it, reserving about 1 cup (250 mL) cooking liquid. Return the cooked pasta to the pan along with the reserved liquid. Spoon the pasta into serving bowls and pour some sauce over each bowl. Pass Parmesan cheese at the table.

Breaded Sole with Tartar Sauce

Serves 6

Tartar sauce is much better when it is homemade. You can put the sauce together while the fish is in the oven. It will also keep for several weeks in the fridge.

6 to 8 sole fillets
2 eggs
1½ cups (375 mL) dry breadcrumbs or panko
   (Japanese bread crumbs)
¼ teaspoon (1 mL) freshly ground pepper
¼ teaspoon (1 mL) salt

TARTAR SAUCE

1 cup (250 mL) mayonnaise
1 tablespoon (15 mL) capers, chopped
1 dill pickle, finely chopped
2 tablespoons (30 mL) finely chopped
   red onion
2 tablespoons (30 mL) lemon juice
½ teaspoon (2 mL) dried dill or 1 teaspoon
   (5 mL) chopped fresh dill
Salt and freshly ground pepper

Preheat oven to 375F (190C). Line a baking sheet with foil and butter it lightly.

Beat eggs in a shallow bowl or pie plate. Combine breadcrumbs, salt and pepper in another shallow bowl. Dip fillet into egg and then into breadcrumbs. Lay on prepared baking sheet.

Bake the fish for 20 to 25 minutes until firm to the touch.

Meanwhile prepare the Tartar Sauce. Combine the mayonnaise, capers, pickle, onion, lemon juice, dill, salt and pepper in a small bowl. Refrigerate until ready to serve. Pass the sauce at the table.

Cod with Mushrooms & Wine   Serves 6

This dish is all prepared in one pan, making cleanup much easier. Serve with some orzo (rice-shaped pasta).

COD

2 pounds (1 kg) cod fillets
1 pound (500 grams) mushrooms
4 tablespoons (60 mL) butter
2 cloves garlic, mashed
¾ cup (175 mL) white wine
1½ cups (375 mL) vegetable or chicken broth
2 tablespoons (30 mL) balsamic vinegar
3 tablespoons (45 mL) fresh chopped parsley
Salt and freshly ground pepper

ORZO

1½ cups (375 mL) orzo
3 to 4 tablespoons (45 to 60 mL) olive oil
3 tablespoons (45 mL) Parmesan cheese
Salt and freshly ground pepper to taste

Cut the cod fillets into six even serving pieces and set aside. Wash the mushrooms and slice. Heat the butter over medium-high heat in a large skillet. Add the mushrooms and cook, stirring occasionally, until they are well browned. Add the garlic and cook 1 minute more. Add the wine, broth, vinegar and parsley. Bring the mushroom sauce to a boil and reduce the liquid by half. Check seasoning, adding pepper and salt if needed. Turn the sauce down to medium low and place the cod fillets in the pan. Cover and cook until the fish is done. It will take about 10 minutes, depending on the thickness of the fillets.

While fish is cooking, prepare the orzo. Bring a large pot of salted water to the boil and add the orzo. Cook until tender but do not overcook. Drain and stir in the olive oil, Parmesan cheese, salt and pepper.

Serve each fillet on a plate with some sauce spooned over top and orzo on the side.

Stovetop Fish Stew

Serves 6

This easy fish stew can be made in one pot on the stove. You can use any combination of seafood as long as it amounts to 2 to 2½ pounds. The fish cooks quickly, so you can prepare the sauce ahead of time and add the fish about 10 to 15 minutes before serving. Rice and a green salad go well with this.

¼ cup (60 mL) olive oil
2 medium onions, diced
1 green or yellow pepper, diced
2 cloves garlic, mashed
1 - 28-ounce (796 mL) can diced tomatoes
2 tablespoons (30 mL) tomato paste
½ cup (125 mL) red wine

1 teaspoon (5 mL) oregano
½ teaspoon (2 mL) basil
½ teaspoon (2 mL) salt
½ teaspoon (2 mL) freshly ground pepper
¾ pound (340 grams) salmon
¾ pound (340 grams) red snapper
¾ to 1 pound (340 to 450 grams) prawns

In a large heavy saucepan, sauté onions and pepper in olive oil over medium heat for 5 to 10 minutes. Add the garlic and cook 1 minute more. Add the tomatoes, tomato paste, wine, oregano, basil, salt and pepper. Bring the sauce to a boil, turn down the heat and simmer 10 to 15 minutes.

Cut fish into 1-inch (2 cm) pieces, removing any skin and bones. Remove tails or shells from prawns if required. Add seafood to heated tomato sauce, stirring gently to coat. Heat on low heat for 15 to 20 minutes or until fish is cooked through. Be careful not to boil or stir vigorously as the fish will fall apart.

Often a recipe calls for only 2 or 3 tablespoons of tomato paste. You can save the remaining paste from the can by rolling it up in plastic wrap and freezing it.

Fish Cakes with Chipotle Mayonnaise

Serves 6

The chipotle mayonnaise is rather spicy and goes well with these mild fish cakes. I use the extra mayonnaise in sandwiches for school lunches.

FISH CAKES

1 pound (500 grams) cod or other white fish
Salt and freshly ground pepper
1 medium onion
2 medium potatoes, scrubbed clean
    (about 12 ounces/375 grams total)
2 cloves garlic, mashed
2 tablespoons (30 mL) chopped parsley
1 tablespoon (15 mL) chopped fresh dill or
    1 teaspoon (5 mL) dried dill
2 tablespoons (30 mL) flour
¾ teaspoon (3 mL) salt
½ teaspoon (2 mL) freshly ground pepper
3 eggs, lightly beaten
½ cup (125 mL) sunflower oil

CHIPOTLE MAYONNAISE

1 chipotle pepper in adobo sauce
1 cup (250 mL) mayonnaise
2 tablespoons (30 mL) lemon juice
2 tablespoons (30 mL) olive oil
¼ cup (60 mL) chopped cilantro
1 clove garlic, minced
¼ teaspoon (1 mL) salt

CHIPOTLE PEPPERS come in a can packed in adobo sauce. When only one is needed for a recipe, set the remaining peppers on a sheet of wax paper, separating them so they do not touch each other. Freeze until firm and store in a labelled container.

Place cod in a saucepan along with about ¾-inch (1.5 cm) water. Sprinkle with a pinch of salt and pepper. Bring to a simmer and cook for 5 minutes, covered. Remove from heat and let sit, uncovered, another 5 minutes. Remove fish from cooking liquid and when cool enough to handle crumble into a large bowl, removing any bones.

Peel and quarter onion. In a food processor fitted with a grater attachment, grate the onion. Drain the juice from the onion in a sieve set over a bowl.

Use the back of a spoon to push out any liquid. Add the onions to the bowl with the fish. Without washing the processor, grate the potatoes. Use your hands to squeeze out any liquid from the potatoes. Add potatoes, garlic, parsley, dill, flour, salt and pepper and eggs to the fish mixture. Mix together well and shape into cakes of roughly 2½-inch (7 cm) diameter. Refrigerate if not cooking immediately.

Prepare the chipotle mayonnaise. Place the chipotle pepper in the food processor attachment of a small handheld blender. Add the remaining ingredients and process to combine.

Cook the fish cakes in 3 batches. Heat 2 to 3 tablespoons (30 to 45 mL) oil in a large skillet over medium heat. Cook about four fish cakes at a time. Let them brown for 2 to 3 minutes before turning over and cooking another 2 to 3 minutes. Keep cooked fish cakes in a warm oven while the rest are cooking. Serve with the chipotle mayonnaise. Store any leftover mayonnaise in a jar in the fridge.

Dijon and Pecan Salmon

Serves 6

The Dijon mustard and honey make a tasty combination of flavours for salmon. The pecans give it a crunchy coating.

2 to 2½ pounds (1 to 1.5 kg) salmon, cut into 6 pieces
⅓ cup (75 mL) butter, melted
3 tablespoons (45 mL) Dijon mustard
2 tablespoons (30 mL) honey
1 cup (250 mL) dried breadcrumbs

¾ cup (175 mL) chopped pecans
1 teaspoon (5 mL) dried oregano or 1 tablespoon (15 mL) chopped fresh rosemary
½ teaspoon (2 mL) salt
¼ teaspoon (1 mL) freshly ground pepper

Preheat oven to 400F (200C).

Combine butter, Dijon mustard and honey in a shallow dish. Combine breadcrumbs, pecans, oregano or rosemary, salt and pepper in another shallow bowl. Pat salmon pieces dry on some paper towel.

Lightly butter an ovenproof dish that will hold all of the salmon pieces in a single layer. Dip each piece of salmon into the Dijon mixture and then roll in the crumb mixture. Place in baking dish. Bake 20 to 25 minutes until salmon is firm to the touch.

Crusted Red Snapper with Tomato Sauce

Serves 6

You could substitute any white fish for this dish.

2 pounds (1 kg) snapper fillets
¾ cup (175 mL) dry breadcrumbs
½ cup (125 mL) Parmesan cheese
½ cup (125 mL) chopped fresh herbs,
    mostly parsley

2 eggs, lightly beaten

TOMATO SAUCE

2 tablespoons (30 mL) olive oil
2 shallots or ½ medium onion, diced fine
1 to 2 garlic cloves, mashed
1 – 28-ounce (796 mL) can diced tomatoes
½ teaspoon (2 mL) sugar
½ teaspoon (2 mL) basil
½ teaspoon (2 mL) oregano
Salt and freshly ground pepper

6 tablespoons (90 mL) olive oil

Cut the fish into serving-size pieces. Lay some wax paper on a plate. Remove any bones from fish with tweezers. Combine breadcrumbs, Parmesan and chopped herbs in a shallow dish. Beat eggs in another shallow dish. Dip each fillet in the egg and then in the crumb mixture. Lay on plate with wax paper.

Meanwhile prepare tomato sauce. In a medium saucepan, heat olive oil and add shallot or onion. Cook over medium heat until soft and beginning to brown, about 5 minutes. Add the garlic and cook an additional minute. Add the tomatoes, sugar, basil, oregano, salt and pepper. Simmer sauce 10 minutes. Transfer to a small serving bowl to pass at the table.

Fry the fish in 2 batches. Heat 3 tablespoons (45 mL) olive oil in a large skillet over medium heat. Lay half of the coated fish fillets in the hot oil. Let the fish cook for 3 to 4 minutes before turning over. This will allow a nice brown crust to form. Turn the fillets over and cook an additional 3 to 4 minutes on the other side.

Keep fillets warm in a 250F (120C) oven while the others are cooking.

pasta

In recent years we have been encouraged to cut down on our intake of carbohydrates. Many people have drastically reduced the amount of pasta they eat. It is important to remember, however, that carbohydrates are essential for growing bodies. Children love pasta and it fills the bottomless pits some of them have for stomachs. Pasta dishes are versatile; some of them can be made at the last minute while others can be prepared well in advance and frozen.

Beef Ragoût over Pasta

Serves 6

The rich flavours in this dish are developed through slow cooking on low heat. It is important to make the ragoût one or two days ahead so that the sauce can sit in the fridge overnight. When the fat is hardened, it can easily be taken off the top. Prepare it on the weekend for a weeknight meal.

3 pounds (1.5 kg) beef short ribs
Salt and freshly ground pepper
2 tablespoons (30 mL) vegetable oil
2 medium onions, chopped
3 carrots, peeled and chopped
3 stalks celery, chopped
4 cloves garlic, mashed
3 bay leaves

4 cups (1 L) beef broth
1⅓ cups (325 mL) red wine
1 – 28-ounce (796 mL) can whole or diced tomatoes, puréed with a handheld blender

6 cups (1.5 L) penne pasta

In a large heavy pot with a lid, heat the oil over medium high heat and brown the short ribs on all sides. Season ribs with salt and pepper. Remove the ribs to a plate, or set them in the up-turned lid of the pot. One less dish to wash!

Pour off all but 1 tablespoon (15 mL) of the fat. Add the onions, carrots and celery to the pot and cook over medium heat, stirring occasionally until vegetables are softened, about 6 to 8 minutes. Add the garlic and cook an additional minute. Add the bay leaves, broth, wine and tomatoes and bring the mixture to a boil. Reduce heat to low and place the browned ribs back in the pot. Simmer the ribs on low for about 2½ hours.

When they are done, transfer the ribs to a cutting board and chop up the meat, removing any fat or gristle. Store the meat in a sealed container in the fridge for 1 to 2 days until ready to serve.

Place the sauce in the fridge to harden the fat. About 1 hour before serving the meal, remove the hardened fat from the sauce and bring the sauce to a boil. You will want to reduce the sauce down to about 5 cups (1.25 L). This will take 10 to 15 minutes of boiling. Stir occasionally. Turn the heat down to medium low and add the chopped meat to the sauce. Heat through.

Meanwhile cook penne according to package directions. Drain and stir in a little oil and salt. Serve the ragoût over the pasta.

Pad Thai with Prawns (or Chicken)

Serves 6

I like to make Pad Thai on one of those days when it's four o'clock and I don't know what to make for dinner, nor do I want to go to the store. I usually have a bag of prawns in the freezer and rice noodles in the pantry. The bean sprouts and cilantro in this dish are really nice, but you can omit them if you like. Some people who claim they don't like cilantro just love this dish. If my kids knew there was fish sauce in this dish they probably wouldn't eat it. They'll never know.

This dish can also be made with chicken. Use two or three boneless, skinless breasts. Slice them thinly on the diagonal and season with salt and pepper. Stir-fry them in the oil to replace the prawns.

1 pound (500 grams) frozen raw prawns, thawed and peeled
1 pound (500 grams) medium-wide rice noodles
2 to 3 tablespoons (30 to 45 mL) fish sauce
½ cup (125 mL) ketchup
2 tablespoons (30 mL) molasses
2 to 3 tablespoons (30 to 45 mL) sugar
¼ cup (60 mL) soy sauce
½ cup (125 mL) water
2 tablespoons (30 mL) sweet chili sauce

¼ teaspoon (1 mL) hot sauce
⅓ cup (75 mL) sunflower oil
4 cloves garlic, mashed
3 eggs, lightly beaten
2 cups (500 mL) bean sprouts
1 bunch green onions, chopped
2 carrots, peeled and grated
¾ cup (175 mL) chopped cilantro
½ cup (125 mL) chopped roasted peanuts
1 lime, cut into wedges for garnish

Set the frozen prawns in a colander over a bowl to thaw. Peel them and set them aside. Place the noodles in a very large bowl (I like to break them in half). Cover with hot but not boiling water and let sit 30 minutes.

Meanwhile prepare the sauce. In a small bowl combine the fish sauce, ketchup, molasses, sugar, soy sauce, water, sweet chili sauce and hot sauce.

Drain the noodles and set aside. Heat 2 tablespoons (30 mL) oil in a large skillet or wok over medium to medium-high heat; stir-fry the prawns for 1 to 2 minutes until cooked through. Remove from pan with a slotted spoon and set aside. Add the garlic and cook it until it is golden. It will only take a few seconds. Add the beaten eggs and cook them, stirring constantly, until dry. Remove eggs from skillet to the bowl with the prawns. Heat remaining oil in the skillet; add the drained noodles to the pan. Stir-fry the noodles over medium heat until they become shiny, 4 to 5 minutes. Add the prawns, eggs, bean sprouts, green onions, carrots, ½ cup (125 mL) of the cilantro and the sauce. Stir to heat through.

Turn Pad Thai out onto a platter and garnish with the remaining ¼ cup (60 mL) of cilantro, chopped peanuts and lime wedges.

Honey Garlic Sausage and Penne

Serves 8

Quick and easy family dinner—no pre-cooking of pasta required! This is the family-sized version of the Community Meal recipe (see page 185). You can substitute Italian sausage.

2 pounds (6 to 8) honey garlic sausages,
    cut in ½-inch (1 cm) pieces
2 medium onions, chopped
3 garlic cloves, mashed
1 teaspoon (5 mL) dried basil
1 teaspoon (5 mL) dried oregano
¼ teaspoon (1 mL) crushed red pepper
    (optional)

2 tablespoons (30 mL) cornstarch
2½ cups (625 mL) milk
2 – 28-ounce (796 mL) cans
    diced tomatoes
4½ cups (1.1 L) penne pasta, uncooked
¾ cup (175 mL) grated Parmesan cheese

In a large heavy saucepan cook sausages on medium-high heat until browned. Drain fat if necessary. Add onions, dried herbs and crushed red pepper. Cook until onion is tender. Add garlic, cook 1 minute.

Stir in cornstarch. Add milk. Stir until mixture comes to a boil and thickens.

Add tomatoes and uncooked penne. Stir well. Return to boil. Cover and reduce heat to simmer. Cook for about 20 minutes or until the pasta is tender. Stir in cheese and serve.

Beef and Macaroni Pie

Serves 10 to 12

*This recipe is large. You can cut it in half if you like, but why not make
the whole recipe and freeze some, or give it to a friend who could use
a homemade meal? My kids don't like cottage cheese so I hide it by
mixing it in the food processor with the eggs. They are none the wiser!*

4 cups (1 L) macaroni
2 medium onions, chopped
3 pounds (1.5 kg) lean ground beef
4 cloves garlic, mashed
1 teaspoon (5 mL) dried oregano
1 teaspoon (5 mL) dried basil
½ teaspoon (2 mL) cinnamon
2 – 28-ounce (796 mL) cans plum tomatoes,
    puréed with a handheld blender
2 tablespoons (30 mL) tomato paste
Salt and freshly ground pepper
½ cup (125 mL) chopped parsley

2 tablespoons (30 mL) soft butter
¼ cup (60 mL) dried breadcrumbs
1 ½ cups (375 mL) grated Parmesan cheese

SAUCE
¼ cup (60 mL) butter
¼ cup (60 mL) flour
2 cups (500 mL) milk
2 cups (500 mL) cottage cheese
2 eggs
Pinch nutmeg
Salt and white pepper

In a large heavy pot combine onions and beef and cook
over medium heat, stirring often, until meat is no longer
pink. Drain fat. Add garlic and spices and cook an additional
minute. Add canned tomatoes and tomato paste. Bring
mixture to a boil, stirring often; turn heat to low and
cook 30 to 40 minutes. Season with salt and pepper.
Add chopped parsley.

Meanwhile, cook macaroni in a pot of boiling salted
water according to package directions. Drain and rinse
in cold water so that it doesn't stick together.

Generously butter 2 shallow glass or ceramic casserole pans with the
2 tablespoons butter. This recipe will make two 13 x 9 x 2-inch (3.5 L) pans,
or you can use 1 large lasagne pan and a smaller 10-inch (25 cm) pie plate.

Shake breadcrumbs over the bottom of the buttered pans. Put a shallow
layer of macaroni on the bottom of each pan. Next put a layer of meat sauce,

dividing it between the 2 pans. Sprinkle the meat with half the Parmesan cheese, reserving the rest for the tops. Cover meat with the remaining macaroni.

Prepare the sauce. In a medium saucepan melt the butter; add the flour and cook for 1 to 2 minutes without browning. Add the milk, stirring frequently while bringing mixture to a boil. Meanwhile in the bowl of a food processor fitted with the metal blade, combine cottage cheese and eggs. When the sauce has thickened, remove from heat and add cottage cheese mixture. Stir well and season with nutmeg, salt and pepper. Pour an equal layer of sauce over each casserole. Sprinkle tops with remaining Parmesan cheese.

If you are freezing the casserole, or serving it later, cover top with wax paper and wrap well in plastic wrap. To bake the thawed casserole, place in preheated 350F (180C) oven. A large 13 x 9 x 2-inch (3.5 L) pan will take about 1 hour. Smaller pans will take about 45 minutes. The casserole should be bubbly around the edges and browned on top.

Pasta with Tomato Cream Sauce

Serves 6

This is the easiest dinner in the world, a favourite in our family.

1 – 24-ounce (700 mL) jar tomato sauce
½ cup (125 mL) cream
1 pound (500 grams) pasta
Parmesan cheese

Heat the tomato sauce and cream in a small saucepan. Cook the pasta in a pot of boiling salted water. Serve with Parmesan cheese and veggie tray. Done!

WITH BACON

Chop 1 pound (500 grams) bacon into ½-inch (1 cm) pieces. Cook until crisp. Drain on paper towel. Pass at the table in a bowl to sprinkle over the pasta.

Beef Lasagne

Serves 10 to 12

Lasagne is a fair amount of work, but because it freezes so well it is great to take away on a boat trip or a ski holiday. The size of the pan I use is 9 x 14 x 2½ inches. I buy lasagne noodles that don't require pre-cooking. This cuts down on the amount of work considerably. You can make the meat sauce a day or two before assembling the dish.

MEAT SAUCE

4 pounds (2 kg) ground beef
3 onions, chopped
4 garlic cloves, mashed
3 – 28-ounce (796 mL) cans diced or
   whole tomatoes (puréed with a handheld
   blender to remove the chunks)
1 tablespoon (15 mL) dried basil
2 tablespoons (30 mL) dried oregano
1 teaspoon (5 mL) freshly ground pepper
2 teaspoons (10 mL) salt
1 tablespoon (15 mL) sugar
1 – 6-ounce (175 mL) can tomato paste

WHITE SAUCE

½ cup (125 mL) butter
½ cup (125 mL) flour
6 cups (1.5 L) milk
1 teaspoon (5 mL) salt
½ teaspoon (2 mL) white pepper
¼ teaspoon (1 mL) ground nutmeg

1 pound (500 grams) box of no-cook
   lasagne noodles

¾ pound (375 grams) Mozzarella
   cheese, grated
2 cups (500 mL) grated Parmesan cheese

To prepare the meat sauce, in a large heavy pot brown the beef with the onions until the beef is no longer pink. Add the garlic and cook 1 to 2 minutes. Add the tomatoes, basil, oregano, pepper, salt, sugar and tomato paste. Bring to boil, turn down heat and simmer 30 to 45 minutes.

To prepare the white sauce, in a medium heavy saucepan, melt butter, add flour and cook without browning for a few minutes. Add milk and seasonings. Slowly bring to a boil and simmer for a few minutes to thicken without burning.

Preheat oven to 350F (180C).

To assemble lasagne, line the bottom of a buttered lasagne pan with about ½ cup (125 mL) white sauce. Lay a single layer of noodles over top. Spread about 2 cups (500 mL) meat sauce on noodles. Top with ½ to ¾ cup (125 to 175 mL) white sauce and then ⅓ cup (75 mL) Parmesan. Repeat layers starting with noodles and ending with white sauce. You should get about 4 layers. Spread Mozzarella and remaining Parmesan over top.

Bake for 1 to 1½ hours. Let sit 10 minutes before serving.

This dish can be covered and refrigerated or frozen. If frozen, thaw before baking. It will take 2 days to thaw in the fridge.

Macaroni and Cheese   Serves 8

This is Maggie's favourite dinner. We serve it with boiled European wieners and salad. The casserole can be made a day or two ahead. If you have an ovenproof pot, you can boil the pasta in the pot. While the pasta is draining, make the sauce in the same pot, return the pasta to the pot and bake it. If you want to freeze it, do so before baking it.

4 cups (1 L) macaroni
¼ cup (60 mL) butter
¼ cup (60 mL) flour
3½ cups (875 mL) milk
1½ tablespoons (22 mL) Dijon mustard

1 teaspoon (5 mL) salt
½ teaspoon (2 mL) freshly ground pepper

6 cups (1.5 L) grated sharp Cheddar cheese

Preheat oven to 350F (180C).

Cook macaroni in a large heavy ovenproof pot with salted water until al dente. Drain in colander and rinse macaroni with cold water to prevent it from sticking.

Using the same pot, melt the butter, stir in the flour. Cook 1 minute. Slowly whisk in the milk. Carefully bring to a boil, whisking constantly. Season the sauce with mustard, salt and pepper. Remove from heat and stir in 4 cups (1 L) of the Cheddar cheese.

Add cooked pasta to sauce and stir well. Taste for seasoning. Smooth top with a rubber spatula, scraping any sauce from around the sides of the pot. Sprinkle remaining 2 cups (500 mL) cheese over top. Bake in oven for 30 to 40 minutes or cool and refrigerate. It will take about 50 minutes to re-heat from the fridge.

Pasta with Pesto Sauce

Serves 6

Pesto sauce freezes well, so make lots and freeze it when basil is in season. This is one of the fastest dinners to prepare. Often we have pasta with pesto sauce on a Sunday night when we arrive home after a weekend away. You can defrost frozen sauce on low in the microwave. You will need about 1½ cups (375 mL) pesto sauce to feed 6 people.

PESTO SAUCE

4 cups (1 L) fresh basil leaves, packed
2 garlic cloves, peeled
⅓ cup (75 mL) pine nuts
1 teaspoon (5 mL) salt
½ teaspoon (2 mL) freshly ground pepper
½ cup (125 mL) grated Parmesan
¾ cup (175 mL) olive oil

PASTA

1 pound (500 grams) fettuccine or linguine noodles
1 teaspoon (5 mL) salt

For the freshest Pesto Sauce, prepare it while the pasta is cooking. If you are freezing the pesto, it should be frozen as soon as it is made.

Use a food processor fitted with the metal blade. With the processor running, drop the garlic through the feed tube to mince. Stop the machine. Add basil, pine nuts, salt, pepper and Parmesan. Pulse several times using on/off motion. With the machine running, pour the oil through the feed tube. Serve or freeze immediately.

To freeze the pesto, put it in an airtight container. Place a thin layer of plastic wrap over the top so that the air doesn't get at it. This will prevent it from discolouring.

To prepare the pasta, bring a large pot of salted water to the boil. Add the pasta, breaking it in half if desired. Cook according to package directions. Reserve about ½ cup (125 mL) of cooking water. Drain pasta and quickly return it to the pot along with the cooking water and the pesto sauce. Toss well. Serve immediately so that it doesn't get cold or lose the bright green colour. Pass freshly grated Parmesan at the table.

Spaghetti with Meat Sauce

Serves 8

This has been a long-time favourite in our house. I often make a double batch of sauce and freeze it in two-, three- or four-serving containers. It's easy to heat up later on one of those nights when everyone is coming and going and needs a last-minute meal. Just put the frozen chunk of sauce in a heavy saucepan, set the heat on low and put on the lid. It won't take long to defrost.

1½ pounds (750 grams) ground beef
1 large onion, finely chopped
2 cloves garlic, mashed
2 – 28-ounce (796 mL) can whole or diced tomatoes
3 tablespoons (45 mL) tomato paste
1 teaspoon (5 mL) dried basil

1 teaspoon (5 mL) dried oregano
1½ teaspoons (7 mL) salt
1 teaspoon (5 mL) sugar
½ teaspoon (2 mL) freshly ground pepper

1 pound (500 grams) spaghetti noodles

Put the beef and onions in a large heavy pot set on medium heat. Cook, breaking up the beef until it is no longer pink and the onions are soft. Add the garlic and cook 1 minute more.

Open the cans of tomatoes and purée them for a few seconds with a handheld blender right in the can, or use a regular blender. Add the tomatoes to the meat along with the tomato paste, basil, oregano, salt, sugar and pepper. If you have fresh herbs double the amount; for example, instead of 1 teaspoon (5 mL) dried, use 2 teaspoons (10 mL) fresh. Bring to a boil, turn down heat and simmer the sauce for 30 to 45 minutes. Check for seasoning.

Bring a large pot of salted water to a boil. Add spaghetti noodles. When the pasta is cooked, drain, return to pan with 2 tablespoons (30 mL) olive oil, and stir well. The pots can sit on the counter for people to heat up some pasta and sauce when they are ready to eat.

Chicken and Pasta Salad with Basil Dressing

Serves 6

If you have barbecued chicken one night, cook extra so you can have pasta salad the next night.

3 cups (750 mL) penne pasta
¾ pound (375 grams) asparagus
1 red pepper, diced
4 to 6 green onions, chopped
1½ cups (375 mL) cooked chopped
   chicken

BASIL DRESSING

1 cup (250 mL) loosely packed fresh basil
1 green onion, white part only, chopped
2 tablespoons (30 mL) balsamic vinegar
½ teaspoon (2 mL) salt
¼ teaspoon (1 mL) freshly ground pepper
2 tablespoons (30 mL) mayonnaise
⅓ cup (75 mL) olive oil

Cook the pasta according to package directions in salted water, being careful not to overcook it. Drain under cold water to stop cooking and cool pasta.

Break the tough stalks off the bottom of the asparagus. Cut each asparagus spear on the diagonal into about 3 pieces. Blanche the asparagus in a small pot of boiling salted water for 2 to 4 minutes depending on how thick the spears are. Drain and rinse under cold water.

Place the chopped red pepper, green onion, chicken, drained asparagus and cooked pasta in a large bowl. Combine all the dressing ingredients in a blender. Pour over salad and toss to combine. Taste for seasoning and add more salt and pepper if desired.

Chicken Tetrazzini

Serves 6 to 8

This dish can be made a day ahead, or it can be frozen. The mushroom soup acts as a stabilizer in this dish but it can be omitted if you prefer. 1-inch (2 cm) pieces of asparagus or broccoli, blanched in boiling water for a minute and rinsed in cold water, could replace the mushrooms. Stir in the asparagus or broccoli when you stir in the chicken.

1 pound (500 grams) mushrooms, sliced
2 medium onions, chopped
3 tablespoons (45 mL) butter
3 cloves garlic, mashed

5 to 6 boneless skinless chicken breasts, cubed
1 tablespoon (15 mL) butter

1 pound (500 grams) fettuccine noodles

SAUCE

¼ cup (60 mL) butter
¼ cup (60 mL) flour
2 cups (500 mL) chicken broth
1 cup (250 mL) milk
1 – 10-ounce (284 mL) can condensed cream of mushroom soup, undiluted
1 tablespoon (15 mL) chopped fresh rosemary
Salt and freshly ground pepper
⅔ cup (150 mL) grated Parmesan cheese

Sauté mushrooms and onions in 3 tablespoons (45 mL) butter until beginning to brown. Add the garlic and cook a few more minutes. Transfer to a large bowl. Sauté chicken in 1 tablespoon (15 mL) of butter until cooked and browned. Transfer chicken to the bowl with the mushrooms. If you prefer, you can poach the chicken in a 350F (180C) oven with ¼ cup (60 mL) white wine and some salt and pepper for about 40 minutes. Use the poaching liquid in the sauce to replace some of the broth. Cool and cube chicken.

For the sauce, melt ¼ cup (60 mL) butter in a medium heavy saucepan. Add flour and cook 1 to 2 minutes. Slowly add broth and milk, whisking constantly. Bring sauce to boil adding can of soup, rosemary and ⅓ cup (75 mL) Parmesan cheese. Season with salt and pepper.

Bring a large pot of salted water to a boil. Break noodles in half and cook until al dente. Drain and rinse with cold water to prevent sticking. Add noodles to chicken and stir in sauce. Pour into a buttered 9 x 13 x 2 inch (3.5 L) ovenproof pan. Sprinkle with additional ⅓ cup (75 mL) Parmesan cheese. Bake 30 to 40 minutes until bubbly.

Pasta with Tomato Sauce

Serves 6

This is what we eat when all of a sudden it's six o'clock and I haven't planned dinner. This tomato sauce is easy to make and only needs to simmer for about 20 minutes.

2 medium onions diced
2 cloves garlic, mashed
2 tablespoons (30 mL) olive oil
2 – 28-ounce (796 mL) cans whole or
    diced tomatoes

1 teaspoon (5 mL) salt
½ teaspoon (2 mL) freshly ground pepper
2 teaspoons (10 mL) sugar
1 teaspoon (5 mL) dried basil
1 teaspoon (5 mL) dried oregano

Heat the olive oil in a medium heavy saucepan. Add the onions and cook until soft without browning, about 5 minutes. Add the garlic and cook another minute.

Using a handheld blender, chop the tomatoes in a bowl. Add them to the onion and garlic. Turn up the heat to medium high adding the salt, pepper, sugar, basil and oregano. When the sauce comes to a boil, turn down the heat and simmer for about 20 minutes.

1 pound (500 grams) pasta
1 teaspoon (5 mL) salt
Parmesan cheese for serving

Bring a large pot of salted water to a boil. Add the pasta and cook according to package directions. Drain and serve with hot tomato sauce and Parmesan cheese.

Be sure to use diced or whole tomatoes. If you buy the crushed tomatoes the sauce will be too thick and dry.

cookies & squares

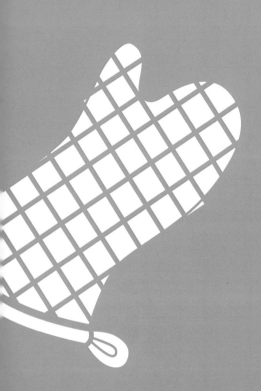

*I love to bake but baked goods don't.
last long around my house. I prefer
to bake in large quantities and freeze
some for school lunches, or just to pull
out when I don't have time to bake.
It seems we are always providing
snacks for a soccer game or other
event and it's good to have home
baking on hand. I hate to buy cookies
because of all the packaging and
additives.*

Lemon Squares

Makes 20 squares

We made lemon squares almost every day at The Cooking Company. *They are also a nice addition to an assortment of baking for a meeting or function, a good way to balance out all of the chocolaty things I like best. If you don't have a food processor, use a pastry cutter to combine the ingredients for the base; whisk the ingredients for the topping in a bowl.*

PASTRY BASE

2 cups (500 mL) flour
½ cup (125 mL) sugar
1 cup (250 mL) cold butter,
   cut in 1-inch (2 cm) cubes

TOPPING

4 eggs
2 cups (500 mL) sugar
¼ cup (60 mL) flour
1 teaspoon (5 mL) baking powder
Zest and juice of 1 lemon

Preheat oven to 350F (180C). Butter a 13 x 9 x 2-inch (3.5 L) pan.

In the bowl of a food processor fitted with a metal blade combine flour, sugar and butter. Pulse until mixture resembles coarse meal. Pour into prepared pan and press down, covering the bottom of the pan evenly. Bake for 10 minutes.

In the same food processor bowl, combine eggs, sugar, flour, baking powder, lemon zest and juice. Pulse once or twice to combine. When the base comes out of the oven, pour lemon mixture over it and return to oven for 25 minutes more, or until centre is set and the edges are light golden.

Cool before slicing. Use a sharp knife dipped in hot water to slice into squares.

SILICONE LINERS — I use silicone-coated liners on my baking sheets. They prevent cookies from sticking to the pans and they make cleanup much easier. They are available in any cooking shop. Although they are rather expensive, they are a good investment if you do a lot of baking. Make sure you buy liners the exact size of your pans.

Cinnamon Almond Cookies

Makes about 10 dozen cookies

This recipe makes a large quantity of dough. If you don't need all of it, freeze half. For last minute entertaining, you can slice the cold dough into cookies and pop them in the oven for a quick dessert. Serve them with a store-bought sorbet or homemade fruit salad.

3 cups (750 mL) all-purpose flour
2 teaspoons (10 mL) ground cinnamon
1 teaspoon (5 mL) allspice
½ teaspoon (2 mL) baking soda
½ teaspoon (2 mL) baking powder
¼ teaspoon (1 mL) salt
1 cup (250 mL) butter, room temperature
¾ cup (175 mL) sugar
¾ cup (175 mL) golden brown sugar, packed
1 large egg
1 large egg yolk
1 teaspoon (5 mL) vanilla extract
1¾ cups (425 mL) sliced almonds, skin on

Mix flour, cinnamon, allspice, baking soda, baking powder and salt in a medium bowl. In another large bowl, beat butter until fluffy. Beat in sugar and golden brown sugar. Add egg and egg yolk, mixing well. Beat in vanilla. Add flour mixture and beat until dough comes together in moist clumps. Add almonds and knead gently in bowl with hands until blended.

Divide dough into 2 equal portions. Roll each into 10-inch-long (25 cm) log, about 1¼ to 1½ inch (3 to 4 cm) in diameter. Wrap dough in plastic wrap and chill for at least 4 hours.

Preheat oven to 350F (180C). Working with 1 log at a time, remove plastic and cut crosswise into ¼-inch (.5 cm) thick rounds. Place rounds on ungreased baking sheet, spacing 1 inch (2 cm) apart.

Bake until light golden brown, about 12 minutes. Transfer cookies to rack and cool completely. Store in an airtight container.

Ginger Snaps

Makes about 4 dozen cookies

This recipe was given to me by our friend Nancy. I swore never to give it to anyone else. Then I made a few changes and got permission from her to share it. If you substitute vegetable shortening for the butter, the resulting cookie will be crisper but you should increase the salt to 1 teaspoon (5 mL).

1½ cups (375 mL) butter, room temperature
1 cup (250 mL) brown sugar
1 cup (250 mL) white sugar
2 eggs
¼ cup (60 mL) corn syrup
¼ cup (60 mL) fancy molasses
3½ cups (875 mL) flour
2 teaspoons (10 mL) ground cloves
1 tablespoon (15 mL) ground ginger
2 teaspoons (10 mL) ground cinnamon
2 teaspoons (10 mL) baking soda
½ teaspoon (5 mL) salt

Preheat oven to 350F (180C). Line baking sheets with parchment paper or silicone liners.

Cream together the butter with the sugars in the bowl of an electric mixer. Add 1 egg at a time, beating well after each addition. Add corn syrup and molasses; mix to combine. Stop machine and then add flour, cloves, ginger, cinnamon, baking soda and salt. Stir on low speed until just combined.

Spoon dough by heaping tablespoons onto prepared baking sheet, spacing at least 2 inches (5 cm) apart. Bake 10 to 12 minutes. Cool on racks. Store in an airtight container.

MOLASSES — Generally we find two kinds of molasses in the grocery store: the darker, stronger-flavoured, less sweet cooking molasses and the milder, lighter and sweeter fancy molasses. I use fancy molasses in most of my baking.

Butter Tart Squares

Makes 16 squares

Butter tart squares are much easier to make than butter tarts.
No rolling out the pastry!

PASTRY BASE
¾ cup (175 mL) flour
¼ cup (60 mL) brown sugar
⅓ cup (75 mL) cold butter

TOPPING
2 eggs
½ cup (125 mL) sugar
½ cup (125 mL) corn syrup
⅛ teaspoon (.5 mL) salt
1 teaspoon (5 mL) vanilla
1 cup (250 mL) raisins
¼ cup (60 mL) flour

Preheat oven to 350F (180C). Butter an 8 x 8 x 2-inch (2 L) square pan.

Combine the flour, brown sugar and butter in a medium bowl and cut together with a pastry cutter. Press this mixture into the bottom of the prepared pan. Bake 12 to 15 minutes.

For topping, use the same mixing bowl. Beat eggs; add sugar, corn syrup, salt, vanilla, raisins and flour. Mix to incorporate flour. Pour over baked crust and return to oven for an additional 25 minutes until set. When cool, cut with a knife dipped in hot water.

Peanut Butter Pinwheel Cookies

Makes 4 to 5 dozen cookies

I have been trying to get this recipe from my mother-in-law Joan for more than 20 years. Finally, when I told her I was writing a cookbook, she agreed to share it. The kids love these cookies and sometimes get a tin of them from their grandmother for their birthdays.

Joan got the recipe from her mum, Nanny Mackie. They both agreed that vegetable shortening produces a crisper cookie and it probably does. I prefer the taste of butter, so I use butter. If you use shortening, increase the salt to 1 teaspoon (5 mL).

1 cup (250 mL) butter, at room temperature
2 cups (500 mL) sugar
1 cup (250 mL) smooth peanut butter
2 eggs
3 cups (750 mL) flour
1 teaspoon (5 mL) baking soda
¼ teaspoon (2 mL) salt

2 cups (250 mL) chocolate chips, melted

Melt the chocolate chips in a bowl set over simmering water. Remove from heat and cool to room temperature.

Cream the butter and sugar together in the bowl of an electric mixer. Add the peanut butter and mix well to incorporate. Add the eggs and mix well. Stop the machine; add the flour, baking soda and salt. Turn the machine back on and mix just until the four is incorporated.

Tear off 4 pieces of wax paper, each about 18 inches (45 cm) long. Lay 1 piece on the counter. Remove half of the peanut butter dough from the bowl and shape it into a rough rectangle in the middle of one sheet of wax paper. Lay another piece of wax paper on top and use a rolling pin to roll the dough out into a large thin rectangle. It should measure about 17 x 11 inches (43 x 28 cm). Carefully remove the top piece of wax paper. With the longer edge of the dough facing you, use a rubber spatula to scrape half the melted chocolate onto dough from end to end. Using a butter spreader, spread the chocolate over the peanut butter dough, making sure it reaches both ends. Leave a 1-inch (2 cm) line with no chocolate at the long end farthest from you. Using the wax paper to help you, begin rolling up the dough, moving it away from you. When you have a long roll, keeping the wax paper over it, transfer it to a baking sheet. Repeat with remaining dough. Chill the rolls for 30 to 60 minutes to make them easier to slice.

Preheat oven to 350F (180C). Remove one roll at a time from the fridge and put it on a cutting board. Use a sharp knife to cut ⅓- to ½-inch (.5 to 1 cm) slices. Don't worry if they are somewhat elongated in shape; they will bake up nicely.

Place them on ungreased baking sheets about 2 inches (5 cm) apart. They will spread. Bake the cookies for 12 to 14 minutes until golden brown. Cool on baking sheets. Store in an airtight container.

Brownies

Makes 20 brownies

Make a double recipe of icing and freeze half for the next batch of brownies. Or, if you prefer, don't bother icing the brownies, just sprinkle them with some icing sugar.

3 eggs
1 cup (250 mL) white sugar
1 cup (250 mL) brown sugar
1 cup (250 mL) butter, melted and cooled
1 teaspoon (5 mL) vanilla
1 cup (250 mL) flour
¾ cup (175 mL) cocoa powder
1 teaspoon (5 mL) baking powder
¾ cup (175 mL) chopped walnuts
    or pecans (optional)

CHOCOLATE ICING
½ cup (125 mL) soft butter
1 cup (250 mL) icing sugar
½ cup (125 mL) cocoa
1 to 2 tablespoons (15 to 30 mL)
    strong coffee

Preheat oven to 350F (180C). Butter a 13 x 9 x 2-inch (3.5 L) pan.

In a large mixing bowl combine eggs, white sugar and brown sugar. Add cooled butter and vanilla. Stir to combine. Sift flour, cocoa and baking powder over butter mixture. Add nuts if desired. Gently stir mixture until combined. Spoon the mixture into prepared pan. Bake 25 minutes. Cool before icing and cutting.

While brownies are baking, prepare the icing. Place butter, icing sugar and cocoa in the bowl of a food processor fitted with a metal blade. Pulse several times to combine. Slowly add coffee through feed tube until icing is a spreading consistency. Spread icing over cooled brownies.

To store the brownies, cover with plastic wrap. They are best eaten fresh, but they will keep for 1 or 2 days at room temperature or in the fridge.

Nana McLennan's Shortbread

Makes 7 to 8 dozen cookies

Nana McLennan was my cousins' other grandmother and she lived to be 103 years old. She made the best shortbread and I have been using her recipe for years. I always use regular salted butter. Berry sugar is slightly finer than regular granulated sugar.

1 pound (500 grams) butter, room temperature
1 cup (250 mL) berry sugar
3½ cups (875 mL) flour

Preheat oven to 325F (160C).

Beat together butter and sugar for 1 to 2 minutes. Add the flour all at once and mix in at low speed. Bring the dough together in a ball.

Have a big clean counter space ready to roll out the dough. Sprinkle the surface with some extra flour. Roll out the dough with a rolling pin. Try to make it as even as possible, about ¼-inch (.5 cm) thick. You can use any kind of cookie cutter; I like to use a 2-inch (5 cm) round. Cut out as many rounds as you can.

Using a spatula, transfer shortbread to a baking sheet, leaving a little space between each one. They won't spread very much. Bring together the remaining dough. Roll it out and cut out more cookies. Repeat until all the dough is used up.

Bake 14 to 18 minutes, watching carefully, until the cookies are a very light golden brown around the edges. Cool on racks. Store in an airtight container. They will keep for 1 or 2 weeks at room temperature. They also freeze well.

Pecan Caramel Squares with Chocolate

Makes 20 squares

These squares are very rich and very good. My husband Gordon makes them every year for a United Way fundraiser at his office. They have become quite popular and fetch a higher price every year.

PASTRY BASE

2½ cups (625 mL) flour
1 cup (250 mL) cold butter, cut in
   1-inch (2 cm) cubes
¾ cup (175 mL) brown sugar

TOPPING

3 cups (750 mL) pecans
1¼ cups (310 mL) butter
1¼ cups (310 mL) brown sugar
½ cup (125 mL) corn syrup
¼ cup (60 mL) whipping cream

1 cup (250 mL) chocolate chips

Preheat oven to 350F (180C). Butter a 13 x 9 x 2-inch (3.5 L) pan.

In the bowl of a food processor fitted with a metal blade, combine flour, 1 cup (250 mL) butter and ¾ cup (175 mL) brown sugar. Pulse several times until mixture resembles a coarse meal. Alternatively, you can combine these ingredients in a mixing bowl with a pastry cutter. Press into bottom of prepared pan. Bake in preheated oven for 10 minutes. Remove from oven and arrange pecans over the top of the baked base.

Meanwhile combine remaining 1¼ cups (310 mL) butter, 1¼ cups (310 mL) brown sugar and corn syrup in a heavy saucepan. Bring to boil and cook on high for 5 to 7 minutes. Remove from heat and add the whipping cream carefully, as the mixture will bubble up. Pour this caramel over the pecans and return pan to oven for 25 minutes more. Remove from oven and immediately sprinkle chocolate chips over the top of the square. Cool completely before slicing with a knife dipped in hot water.

Oatmeal (Raisin) Chocolate Chip Cookies

Makes 2½ to 3 dozen large cookies

This is a chewy cookie. My kids are not wild about raisins so I disguise them by grinding them up.

1 cup (250 mL) butter, room temperature
½ cup (125 mL) white sugar
1 cup (250 mL) brown sugar
2 eggs
1 teaspoon (5 mL) vanilla
1 cup (250 mL) raisins (optional)
1½ cups (375 mL) flour
1 teaspoon (5 mL) baking soda
1 teaspoon (5 mL) ground cinnamon
¼ teaspoon (1 mL) ground nutmeg
½ teaspoon (2 mL) ground allspice
⅛ teaspoon (.5 mL) ground cloves
¼ teaspoon (1 mL) salt
2 cups (500 mL) quick cooking oatmeal
1½ cups (375 mL) chocolate chips

Preheat oven to 350F (180C). Cover the raisins with boiling water. Let sit 5 minutes. Drain well and grind them up in a food processor fitted with a metal blade. The small processor attachment of the handheld blender also works well for this.

In the bowl of an electric mixer, cream the butter and add the white and brown sugars, beating well. Add 1 egg at a time, beating well after each addition. Add the vanilla. Stop the beaters. Add the flour, baking soda, cinnamon, nutmeg, allspice, cloves, salt, oatmeal and chocolate chips. Mix gently until the flour is incorporated, then stir in the raisins just at the end.

Using an ice cream scoop, spoon the dough by heaping tablespoonfuls onto baking sheets, leaving a few inches between each cookie. Push the dough down slightly to flatten.

Bake 10 to 12 minutes until cookies are golden around the outside and cooked in the middle. Cool slightly on pans before transferring to racks.

Chocolate Chip Cookies

Makes about 4 dozen cookies,
depending on how much dough you eat!

*These are plain old-fashioned chocolate chip cookies, nothing fancy
about them. If your butter and eggs are at room temperature, the
cookies will be thinner and crispy. With cold butter and eggs the
cookies will be thicker and chewier.*

1 cup (250 mL) butter, room temperature
1 cup (250 mL) packed brown sugar
½ cup (125 mL) white sugar
2 eggs
1 teaspoon (5 mL) vanilla

2 cups (500 mL) flour
1 teaspoon (5 mL) baking soda
¼ teaspoon (1 mL) salt
1¾ cups (425 mL) chocolate chips

Preheat oven to 350F (180C).

Using an electric mixer, cream the butter and add
brown sugar and white sugar. Add 1 egg at a time.
Add the vanilla. Stop the mixer and place the flour,
baking soda, salt and chocolate chips on top of
the butter mixture. Turn the mixer back on low and
mix until the flour is incorporated. Drop the cookie
dough by heaping tablespoons onto baking sheets,
leaving about 2 inches (5 cm) between each one.
Bake 8 to 10 minutes until golden around the
edges. Store in an airtight container.

Old-Fashioned Date Squares

Makes 20 squares

We sold dozens of date squares at The Cooking Company, *I guess because there is nothing quite like a date square with a cup of tea or coffee. Use pitted dates; it is fine if they are pre-chopped. Old-fashioned rolled oats are not the same as quick cooking. You need the whole oats to give these squares the proper texture.*

DATE MIXTURE

2 cups (500 mL) pitted dates
1 cup (250 mL) orange juice

OAT BASE

1 cup (250 mL) butter, melted
3 cups (750 mL) old-fashioned rolled oats
1½ cups (375 mL) flour
1½ cups (375 mL) brown sugar
1 teaspoon (5 mL) baking soda
1 teaspoon (5 mL) cinnamon

Preheat oven to 350F (180C). Butter a 13 x 9 x 2-inch (3.5 L) pan.

In a small saucepan, cook the dates with the orange juice over medium heat until they are a good spreading consistency. Cool while you prepare the oat base.

Melt the butter in a small saucepan or in the microwave. In a medium bowl, combine the oats, flour, brown sugar, baking soda and cinnamon. Stir in the melted butter and mix well.

Press about two-thirds of the oat mixture into the bottom of the prepared pan. Spread the date mixture over the oats, trying to get it into all the corners. Sprinkle the remaining one-third oat mixture over the dates, pressing down lightly.

Bake about 25 minutes until golden brown around the edges. Cool before cutting into squares.

Oatmeal Lace Cookies

Makes about 4 dozen cookies

This is a beautiful, lacy, rich cookie. The recipe comes from my grandmother.

I used to make dozens of these to sell at the farmers' market on Salt Spring Island when I was a child. The ladies were always asking for my recipe, but my mum would never let me give it out.

This more adult type of cookie is nice served with afternoon tea or with ice cream at the end of a dinner party.

It is important to line the baking sheets with parchment paper and not with silicone liners, otherwise the cookies will stick to the pans. It is also very important for the texture of the cookie to use old-fashioned rolled oats and not quick cooking oats.

2½ cups (625 mL) packed brown sugar
2½ cups (625 mL) old-fashioned rolled oats
1 cup (250 mL) butter, melted and cooled slightly
3 tablespoons (45 mL) flour
1 teaspoon (5 mL) vanilla
1 egg, lightly beaten

Preheat oven to 375F (190C). Line baking sheets with parchment paper.

In a medium bowl combine brown sugar and rolled oats. Pour melted butter over top. Add flour, vanilla and egg. Mix well with a spoon.

These cookies spread right out. Spoon the dough by teaspoonfuls onto the parchment-lined baking sheets. Be sure to leave a good 3 inches (8 cm) between each cookie. You will probably only be able to bake 6 to 8 cookies at a time. Bake the cookies for about 7 minutes, until just starting to go a darker brown around the edges. Remove from oven. Let sit 2 to 3 minutes before removing to a cooling rack. Store them in an airtight container.

desserts

We don't eat dessert every day but usually just have fruit after dinner. I do love to bake desserts, so they are some of my favourite things to take to a party. I like simple things with either lots of fresh fruit or my big weakness, chocolate. The cakes in this chapter make easy desserts.

Pies take time to prepare so there is no point in only making one. Make several and freeze some or give them away. You can freeze an unbaked pie. Cook from frozen at 350F (180C) for about one hour.

Mrs. Love's Blueberry Cake

Makes 20 squares

*This recipe is named after my mother-in-law, who gave me the recipe.
It was a very popular square at* The Cooking Company. *If you don't have
blueberries, use blackberries or chopped apple. Frozen fruit works well and it
doesn't need to be thawed before using. This a great cake to take to a bake sale.*

CAKE

½ cup (125 mL) butter, room temperature
1½ cup (375 mL) sugar
2 eggs
1 cup (250 mL) milk
1 teaspoon (5 mL) vanilla
3 cups (750 mL) flour
2 teaspoons (10 mL) baking powder
¼ teaspoon (1 mL) salt

3 cups (750 mL) blueberries

TOPPING

½ cup (125 mL) cold butter
¾ cup (175 mL) flour
½ cup (125 mL) sugar

Preheat oven to 350F (180C). Butter a 17 x 12 inch (45 x 30 cm) rimmed
baking sheet.

Using an electric mixer beat together butter and sugar until light and fluffy.
Add one egg at a time, beating well after each addition. Scrape down bowl.
Add milk and vanilla and mix lightly. Stop mixer; place flour, baking powder and
salt on top of egg mixture. Turn mixer on low and slowly mix in flour, stopping
machine as soon as the flour is incorporated. Spread the cake batter evenly
over the bottom of the prepared pan. Reserve the mixing bowl for the topping.

Sprinkle the top of the cake evenly with the blueberries. Using the same mixing
bowl, mix the topping ingredients together until crumbly. Sprinkle evenly over
the blueberries. Bake for 25 to 30 minutes until golden brown on top. Cool on
a rack and cut into squares.

Fruit Pies

Makes 1 – 9-inch (23 cm) pie, enough to serve 8

Follow the pastry-making instructions in this recipe for any type of dessert pie.

PASTRY

2 cups (500 mL) flour
¼ cup (60 mL) sugar
1 cup (250 mL) cold butter, diced
4 to 5 tablespoons (60 to 75 mL) ice water

MIXED BERRY FILLING

6 cups (1.5 L) mixed cold berries
1 cup (250 mL) sugar
Pinch of salt
2 tablespoons (30 mL) quick tapioca
2 tablespoons (30 mL) cornstarch

APPLE FILLING

Juice of 1 lemon
5-6 Granny Smith apples, peeled, cored, cut in
   ½ inch (1 cm) chunks
1 cup (250 mL) sugar
½ teaspoon (2mL) cinnamon
Pinch of salt
2 tablespoons quick tapioca

THICKENING — Pie filling has to be thick enough to hold together when the pie is sliced. Instead of flour I use tapioca, or a combination of cornstarch and quick tapioca for juicy fruit. Tapioca is the consistency of coarse salt and works well in holding a pie together.

Start by mixing filling ingredients together being careful not to squish the fruit. (As you chop apples, add them to the lemon juice, stirring frequently). Keep fillings in fridge while you make the pastry.

Have a cup of ice water ready. Place the flour and sugar in a medium bowl and mix lightly. Cut the butter into the flour, using a pastry cutter. The mixture should resemble a coarse meal, all chunks of butter smaller than a pea. Work as quickly as possible so that the butter does not become soft.

Add 3 tablespoons (45 mL) of ice water. Mix the pastry with a fork. Add 1 to 2 tablespoons (15 to 30 mL) water until the pastry comes together in a ball. Use your hands to bring the pastry together, but be careful not to handle it too much because your warm hands will soften the butter. Divide the pastry in half.

Sprinkle some extra flour on the countertop and roll out one half of the pastry. Keep plenty of flour on the pastry so that it doesn't stick to the counter. If you have a 12-inch (30cm) diameter pot lid, plate, or bowl use it as a template to cut the pastry circle. Gently drape the pastry over the rolling pin and transfer it to the pie plate, letting the excess hang over the edge. Prick with a fork and chill.

Preheat the oven to 400F (200C).

Roll out the remaining pastry in the same way. Remove the pie plate from the fridge. Gently place pie filling in the bottom shell. Drape the top round of pastry over the filling and slit a few holes in the top. To seal the 2 edges together, fold over the top edge while grabbing the bottom edge inside the fold. Do this all around the outside edge of the pie and flute the crust with your finger or the blunt end of a fork. Put the whole pie back into the fridge and chill for 15 minutes.

Place the pie on a baking sheet and bake for 15 minutes, then turn the heat down to 350F (180C). Bake 40–50 minutes more until the crust is golden. Don't worry if some of the filling oozes out. Cool the pie for several hours, letting the filling set before slicing.

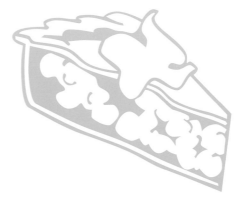

GLAZE — Many recipes call for brushing the pastry with an egg glaze before baking. Maybe I'm just lazy but I find that a good buttery pasty doesn't need a glaze.

Tarte Tatin

Serves 8

This traditional French apple tart is easier to make than you might think. It is a wonderful winter dessert that should be served warm, with vanilla ice cream.

FILLING

½ cup (125 mL) butter
1 cup (250 mL) sugar
¼ cup (60 mL) brandy
Zest of 1 lemon
½ teaspoon (2 mL) ground cinnamon
6 to 7 Granny Smith apples
2 tablespoons (30 mL) lemon juice

PASTRY

1½ cup (375 mL) flour
2 tablespoons (30 mL) sugar
10 tablespoons (150 mL)
   cold butter, cubed
4 to 5 tablespoons (60 to 75 mL)
   cold water

To prepare the filling, melt the butter in a large heavy saucepan or skillet. Add the sugar, brandy, lemon zest and cinnamon. Bring this mixture to a boil and boil for 1 minute; turn off the heat while you prepare the apples. Have a large (10- to 11-inch/25 to 27 cm) pie plate ready.

Peel and core the apples and cut them into eighths. Add them to the caramel filling. Bring caramel back to the boil and turn down heat to medium. Cook the apples in the syrup, stirring occasionally, for 15 to 20 minutes until they start to become a darker golden brown. Add the lemon juice and turn up the heat to high. Cook the apples another 5 to 10 minutes, shaking the pan from time to time. Quickly pour the apples into the pie plate, scraping out all the caramel with a spatula. Be careful not to burn yourself. Let the apple mixture cool in the pan.

Preheat oven to 425F (220C). Prepare the pastry, following the instructions given for Fruit Pies (pages 132–133). When the apple mixture is cool, place a circle of pastry, slightly larger than the pie plate, over the apples, tucking in the edges. Bake the tart 25 to 30 minutes, until the pastry begins to turn golden brown.

As soon as the tart is out of the oven, using oven mitts to avoid burning yourself with hot caramel, place a serving plate on top of the pie plate. Holding both the pie plate and the serving plate with the gloves, quickly invert the tart onto the plate and cool.

Sour Cream Coffee Cake
Serves 10 to 12

This is one of the first things I baked in a high school foods class. I have always loved coffee cake. I think it makes a great after-school snack, and it's also perfect for morning coffee. If you don't want to use sour cream, yogurt works just fine. You can bake this in a regular tube pan or in a decorative non-stick bundt pan. With the bundt pan, you put topping in the bottom of the pan so that when you turn it out the topping will be on the top. With a regular tube pan, you start with the batter and end with the topping.

TOPPING

½ cup (125 mL) brown sugar
½ cup (125 mL) chopped pecans
1½ teaspoons (7 mL) ground cinnamon

CAKE

1¾ cups (425 mL) flour
1½ teaspoons (7 mL) baking powder
½ teaspoon (2 mL) baking soda
½ cup (125 mL) butter, room temperature
1 cup (250 mL) sugar
3 eggs
1½ teaspoons (7 mL) vanilla
1 cup (250 mL) sour cream or plain 2% yogurt

Preheat oven to 350F (180C). Butter a 10-inch (4 L) tube or bundt pan.

Prepare the topping by combining the brown sugar, pecans and cinnamon in a small bowl. Set aside.

Prepare the cake by combining flour, baking powder and baking soda in a small bowl. In another bowl, cream together butter and sugar with an electric mixer. Add 1 egg at a time. Add vanilla and sour cream. Add flour mixture and gently combine without overmixing. If using a decorative bundt pan, sprinkle half of the brown sugar mixture on the bottom of the pan. Add half of the batter and spread evenly. Sprinkle remaining brown sugar mixture over middle. Spread remaining batter over this. If using a tube pan, start with half of the batter; sprinkle half of the brown sugar over top. Then spread the remaining batter over top and add the remaining brown sugar mixture.

Bake in the middle of the preheated oven for about 40 minutes or until a cake tester inserted in the centre comes out clean. Cool on a rack before turning out onto a plate.

Chocolate Pecan Tarts

Makes 36 tarts

At first I wasn't planning on including this recipe, as it is not really a simple one. Another problem is that the authentic European tart tins are not easy to find. The tins I use measure 6.25 cm on the top, 4 cm on the bottom and they are 1.5 cm deep. I bought mine in London in 1981. You can use any tart tins that have approximately the same measurements.

CHOCOLATE PASTRY

2 cups (500 mL) flour
½ cup (125 mL) brown sugar
⅓ cup (75 mL) cocoa
1 cup (250 mL) cold butter, cut in cubes
2 to 3 tablespoons (30 to 45 mL) cold milk

36 whole pecans for garnish

TART FILLING

⅓ cup (75 mL) butter, melted and cooled
1 cup (250 mL) brown sugar
1 cup (250 mL) dark corn syrup
3 large eggs

2¼ cups (560 mL) coarsely chopped pecans
2 cups (500 mL) chocolate chips

Make the chocolate pastry, using a food processor fitted with a metal blade. Add the flour, brown sugar and cocoa to the bowl of the food processor; pulse to combine. Add the cubed butter. Pulse until the butter is incorporated. Slowly add the milk through the feed tube, stopping often to check and see if the pastry will hold together when you squeeze a clump of it. The pastry shouldn't be too wet or it will be difficult to work with. Transfer to a bowl.

Lightly butter 3 one-dozen tart tins. Roll the pastry into balls that measure about 1 tablespoon (15 mL). Using your thumbs, press the pastry over the bottom and up the sides of each tart tin. Try to spread the pastry as evenly as possible. Chill the pastry shells for at least 30 minutes.

Preheat oven to 350F (180C). Roast the 36 whole pecans in preheated oven for about 7 minutes. They are the garnish for the tarts.

Prepare the tart filling by whisking together the melted butter, brown sugar, corn syrup and eggs. Pour the filling into a squeeze bottle or jug so that it is easy to pour over the pastry.

Spoon about 1 tablespoon (15 mL) of chopped pecans into each chilled tart shell. Squeeze or pour filling into the tarts, being careful not to fill them too full. Bake the tarts for 20 to 25 minutes, rotating them half way through so that they cook evenly.

Melt the chocolate chips in a stainless bowl over a pot of simmering water. Spoon a dollop of melted chocolate onto each tart and place a roasted whole pecan on top. Let chocolate set before removing tarts from pans. Use the tip of a sharp knife to loosen the tarts from the tins.

These tarts freeze well.

Carrot Cake with Cream Cheese Icing

Serves 12

This is an old-fashioned recipe for a moist and delicious carrot cake. Open the can of pineapple and set it in a sieve over a bowl to drain well before using.

CARROT CAKE

4 eggs
1 cup (250 mL) sunflower oil
1½ cup (375 mL) brown sugar
1 cup (250 mL) canned crushed pineapple, well drained
2 cups (500 mL) grated carrot
2 cups (500 mL) flour
2 teaspoons (10 mL) baking powder
1½ teaspoons (7 mL) baking soda

1 tablespoon (15 mL) ground cinnamon
1 teaspoon (5 mL) ground allspice
1 teaspoon (5 mL) ground nutmeg

CREAM CHEESE ICING

8 ounces (250 grams) cream cheese, room temperature
4 ounces (125 grams) butter, room temperature
1 cup (250 mL) icing sugar
½ teaspoon (2 mL) vanilla

Preheat oven to 350F (180C). Butter a 13 x 9 x 2-inch (3.5 L) baking pan.

Break eggs into a large bowl. Whisk together well. Add oil and brown sugar and mix well. Add pineapple and carrot and mix well. Fold in the flour, baking powder, baking soda, cinnamon, allspice and nutmeg, being careful not to overmix. Pour into prepared pan and bake about 30 minutes or until centre is set. Cool completely before icing.

When preparing the icing, it is important for the cream cheese and butter to be at room temperature in order for these two ingredients to blend easily.

Beat together cream cheese and butter in a bowl. Add vanilla and sift in the icing sugar, mixing well. Ice the cooled cake.

Chocolate Velvet Mousse

Serves 16

This is a very rich dessert, great for a special occasion. It freezes well, or it can be made several days ahead and kept in the fridge. You can either make it in a 10-inch (3 L) springform pan or in a serving bowl. If you don't need such a large quantity, cut the recipe in half.

For Valentine's Day, make it in a heart-shaped springform pan and serve it with raspberry sauce.

2 pounds (1 kg) bittersweet chocolate (not unsweetened)
6 ounces (170 grams) unsalted butter
1 tablespoon (15 mL) instant espresso granules
1 tablespoon (15 mL) hot water
6 eggs, room temperature
¾ cup (175 mL) icing sugar
¼ cup (60 mL) orange liqueur, such as Grand Marnier
4 cups (1 L) whipping cream

Chop chocolate into chunks and place it with the butter in a stainless steel bowl set over simmering water. Stir occasionally until melted, about 30 minutes. Remove from heat and allow to cool to room temperature, about another 30 minutes. Dissolve the coffee granules in the hot water; cool for 5 minutes.

Carefully separate the eggs so as not to break the yolks: set aside the egg whites in a large dry bowl; place the yolks in another large bowl. Sift the icing sugar over the yolks and mix lightly. Gently mix the liqueur and coffee mixture into the yolks and sugar. Set aside.

Beat the whipping cream until if forms soft peaks. If the cream is whipped too hard, it will be difficult to incorporate. Place the whipped cream in the fridge. Wash and dry the beaters well. Beat the egg whites until they form soft peaks.

With a large serving spoon add the cooled chocolate to the yolk mixture, scraping out the bowl with a rubber spatula. Fold together gently for just a few strokes. Now add the beaten egg whites, folding gently but not completely. Finally add the whipped cream and continue to fold all the mixtures together until they are incorporated.

Pour mixture into a non-stick springform pan or a large serving bowl. Place in fridge to set for at least 6 hours. To freeze, wrap well once it is set; it will keep up to 1 month in the freezer. This dessert can be made two days ahead, covered in plastic wrap and kept in the fridge.

RASPBERRY SAUCE

2 cups (500 mL) raspberries, fresh or frozen (unsweetened, thawed)
3 tablespoons (45 mL) sugar
2 teaspoons (10 mL) lemon juice

Combine sauce ingredients in a blender. Pour through a sieve to remove most of the seeds. Chill until ready to serve. Makes about 1 cup (250 mL).

Sliced Strawberries with Vanilla Sugar and Whipped Cream
Serves 6

Strawberries are available almost any time of the year. This is an easy dessert that can be served after any meal. Brownies would go well with it too.

VANILLA SUGAR

1 cup (250 mL) berry sugar
1 vanilla bean

STRAWBERRIES

2 pounds (1 kg) fresh strawberries
3 tablespoons (45 mL) vanilla sugar
1 cup (250 mL) whipping cream

To make vanilla sugar put the berry sugar into a jar with a tight-fitting lid. Slit the vanilla bean down the middle to expose the tiny vanilla grains; then cut the vanilla bean in half horizontally so it will fit into the jar. Push the vanilla bean into the sugar. Put lid on jar. After several days the sugar will take on the flavour of the vanilla beans. This sugar keeps for months in the pantry.

To prepare the strawberries, rinse them and drain well. Cut off the green tops and slice the strawberries into 3 or 4 pieces. Place in a serving bowl. Sprinkle with about 2 tablespoons (30 mL) of the vanilla sugar and toss to coat. They can be prepared several hours ahead of time and kept in the fridge.

Whip the cream until soft peaks form. Add remaining 1 tablespoon vanilla sugar. Serve a dollop of cream on the strawberries.

Fruit Crumble

Serves 12

Use any combination of fruit for this recipe but keep the proportions the same. Frozen blackberries, blueberries or chopped rhubarb work very well. This is a delicious dessert any time of the year.

6 cups (1.5 L) thick-sliced strawberries
6 cups (1.5 L) peeled and chopped apples
   (½ inch/1 cm)
OR
4 cups (1 L) blueberries
4 cups (1 L) peeled and chopped apples
4 cups (1 L) strawberries

¾ cup (175 mL) sugar
3 tablespoons (45 mL) flour
2 tablespoons (30 mL) lemon juice

CRUMBLE TOPPING

½ cup (125 mL) melted butter
1 cup (250 mL) brown sugar
½ teaspoon (2 mL) ground cinnamon
¾ cup (175 mL) rolled oats
½ cup (125 mL) flour
½ cup (125 mL) chopped pecans (optional)

Preheat oven to 350F (180C).

Prepare the crumble topping by combining the butter, brown sugar, cinnamon, rolled oats, flour and pecans, if using. Set aside.

Combine fruit with the sugar, flour and lemon juice.Transfer fruit to a 13 x 9 x 2-inch (3.5 L) ovenproof dish. Sprinkle crumble topping evenly over top. Bake 45 to 55 minutes until bubbly around the edges.

Cool and serve with vanilla ice cream. You can also freeze a cooked fruit crumble.

Gingerbread Cake with Caramel Sauce

Serves 10

Serve this cake slightly warm with freshly whipped cream and warm caramel sauce. It is the perfect winter dessert.

CAKE

¾ cup (175 mL) butter, at room temperature
½ cup (125 mL) brown sugar
2 eggs
1 cup (250 mL) fancy molasses
3 tablespoons (45 mL) finely chopped
    fresh ginger
2¼ cups (560 mL) flour
2 teaspoons (10 mL) baking soda
2 teaspoons (10 mL) ground ginger
1 cup (250 mL) buttermilk

CARAMEL SAUCE

1 cup (250 mL) packed brown sugar
½ cup (125 mL) butter
½ cup (125 mL) whipping cream

Preheat oven to 350F (180C). Position the rack in the centre of the oven. Butter a 10-inch (3 L) springform pan.

Cream together the butter and the sugar until light and fluffy. Add 1 egg at a time, beating well after each addition. Add the molasses and chopped fresh ginger. Add buttermilk.

Add flour, baking soda and ground ginger, mixing until just incorporated.

Pour batter into prepared pan. Bake about 40 minutes or until cake is set in the centre and a toothpick comes out clean. Cool cake in pan for about 30 minutes before removing.

To prepare the Caramel Sauce, combine brown sugar, butter and whipping cream in a small heavy saucepan. Heat together over low heat until sugar dissolves. Turn up heat and simmer sauce until it thickens, 5 to 10 minutes.

Lemon Loaf

Makes 1 large 5 x 9-inch (14 x 23 cm) loaf

This recipe is from our long-time family friend, Ann, who now lives on Salt Spring Island. The ingredients are similar to those in Lemon Pound Cake but that is a more formal cake, whereas a loaf lends itself to casual eating. I love a slice of lemon loaf with my afternoon tea and a slice is also perfect for school lunches.

LOAF
½ cup (125 mL) butter, room temperature
1 cup (250 mL) sugar
2 eggs
½ cup (125 mL) milk
1½ cups (375 mL) flour
1 teaspoon (5 mL) baking powder
¼ teaspoon (1 mL) salt
Zest of 1 lemon

GLAZE
Juice of 1 lemon
2 tablespoons (30 mL) sugar

Preheat oven to 350F (180C). Butter a 9 x 5 x 3-inch (2 L) loaf pan.

Beat the butter. Add the sugar and beat until light and fluffy. Add 1 egg at a time, beating after each addition. Stir in the milk. All at once add the flour, baking powder, salt and lemon zest. Mix just until the flour is incorporated.

Pour the batter into the prepared loaf pan. Bake 50 to 60 minutes or until a toothpick inserted in the centre comes out clean.

While the loaf is baking, prepare the glaze. Heat the lemon juice and sugar in a small saucepan or in an ovenproof measuring cup in the microwave for 1 minute or until sugar is dissolved. As soon as the loaf comes out of the oven brush it liberally with the hot glaze. Cool in pan. Wrap tightly and store at room temperature This loaf keeps for several days when well wrapped.

Lemon Pound Cake

Serves 10 to 12

This is a great cake to take away for a weekend at a cabin, as it will keep at room temperature for 3 to 5 days.

CAKE

2⅓ cups (575 mL) all-purpose flour
1½ teaspoons (7 mL) baking powder
½ teaspoon (2 mL) baking soda
1¼ cups (310 mL) butter, room temperature
1½ cups (375 mL) sugar
2 large yolks
3 large eggs
1½ teaspoons (7 mL) vanilla
½ cup (125 mL) milk (or buttermilk)
¼ cup (60 mL) lemon juice
1 tablespoon (15 mL) grated lemon zest

LEMON GLAZE

1 cup (250 mL) icing sugar
5 tablespoons (75 mL) lemon juice

Preheat oven to 350F (180C) and set the rack in the bottom third of the oven. Butter a 10-inch (4 L) bundt pan.

In a small bowl, combine flour, baking powder and baking soda. Set aside. In the bowl of an electric mixer, beat butter and sugar at medium speed for about 2 minutes, until light and fluffy. On low speed, beat in one yolk at a time. Add 1 whole egg at a time, beating for about 20 seconds after each one. Scrape down the bowl. Mix in the vanilla. With the mixer running on low speed, add half the flour mixture and mix just until combined. Add the milk, lemon juice and lemon zest; mix until combined. Add the remaining flour mixture, scraping down the bowl, and mix the batter for another 20 seconds. Pour the batter into the prepared pan. Smooth the top. Bake in the middle rack of the oven for 45 to 50 minutes, until a toothpick inserted in the middle comes out clean.

While the cake is baking, make the Lemon Glaze by whisking together the icing sugar and lemon juice in a small bowl. Cool the cake in the pan for about 15 minutes. Invert the cake onto a rack set over a plate to catch the glaze drips. Poke it with a skewer to help absorb the glaze. Liberally brush the cake with the glaze, being sure to cover it completely.

Upside-Down Apple Caramel Cake

Serves 9

This is an easy cake to make because the caramel isn't fussy at all.
Pay special attention to the size of the pan for best results. Don't use
a springform pan, as the caramel may leak through the seam.

CARAMEL TOPPING
¼ cup (60 mL) butter
¾ cup (175 mL) brown sugar
1 tablespoon (15 mL) honey

CAKE
1½ cups (375 mL) flour
2 teaspoons (10 mL) baking powder
1 teaspoon (5 mL) ground ginger

½ teaspoon (2 mL) ground cinnamon
Pinch of salt
2 Granny Smith apples
½ cup (125 mL) butter
1 cup (250 mL) sugar
2 eggs
½ teaspoon (2 mL) vanilla
½ cup (125 mL) milk

Preheat oven to 325F (160C). Butter a 9 x 9 x 2-inch (2.5 L) cake pan.

To make the Caramel Topping, in a saucepan combine the ¼ cup (60 mL) butter, brown sugar and honey. Cook over medium heat until the butter is melted and the mixture is smooth. Pour the caramel into the bottom of the buttered cake pan.

In a small bowl, combine the flour, baking powder, ginger, cinnamon and salt. Have all the remaining cake ingredients ready before cutting the apples so that they don't go brown.

Peel, quarter and core the apples. Cut each quarter into 3 slices. Arrange the apple slices on top of the caramel.

Beat the ½ cup (125 mL) butter in the bowl of an electric mixer. Add the sugar and beat until light and fluffy. Add 1 egg at a time, beating well after each addition. Add the vanilla and the milk and mix well. Add the dry ingredients all at once and mix in lightly just until flour is incorporated. Pour the batter over the apples and smooth out to the edges of the pan. Bake for 45 to 50 minutes until cake is firm when touched in the middle. Remove from oven and cool for 10 minutes in the pan before running a knife around the outside edge of the pan. Place a plate over the cake pan and turn the cake over onto the plate. Let sit for 1 or 2 minutes and then remove the pan. Serve warm with vanilla ice cream.

Pumpkin Pie

Makes 1 – 9-inch (23 cm) pie, enough to serve 8

I like this pumpkin pie recipe because you don't have to pre-bake the crust. Just get it nice and cold in the freezer before adding the filling, then place the unbaked pie on a preheated baking pan.

CRUST

1½ cups (375 mL) flour
2 tablespoons (30 mL) sugar
10 tablespoons (150 mL) cold butter,
    cut in ½-inch (1-cm) dice
3 to 4 tablespoons (45 to 60 mL) ice water

PUMPKIN FILLING

⅔ cup (150 mL) brown sugar
½ cup (125 mL) white sugar
2 tablespoons (30 mL) flour
½ teaspoon (2 mL) salt
½ teaspoon (2 mL) ground cinnamon
½ teaspoon (2 mL) ground allspice
½ teaspoon (2 mL) ground ginger
¼ teaspoon (1 mL) ground cloves
1½ cup (375 mL) solid pack pumpkin
3 eggs
½ cup (125 mL) whipping cream

To prepare the crust, place the flour and sugar in a medium bowl. Add the butter and cut it into the flour with a pastry cutter. When the flour and butter resemble a coarse meal, add 3 tablespoons (45 mL) cold water and mix lightly to bring it all together. Add more water if needed. Form the dough into a ball, wrap in plastic wrap and chill for 30 minutes.

Roll out the crust, following instructions for half of the pastry in Fruit Pies (pages 132–133). Prick the bottom of the crust with a fork and freeze for at least 1 hour.

Preheat oven to 450F (230C). Place a baking pan large enough to hold the pie plate in the oven. To prepare the filling, beat together the brown sugar, white sugar, flour, salt, cinnamon, allspice, ginger and cloves. Add pumpkin, eggs and cream and mix well. Pour the filling into the frozen crust. Place pie on top of the hot baking pan in the oven. This will cook the bottom of the crust. Bake 10 minutes; turn oven down to 325F (160C) and bake an additional 40 minutes, or until the crust is golden brown and the centre is set. Cool on rack. Serve with whipped cream.

Our Favourite Birthday Cake Serves 10 to 12

When I was growing up we always had everyone's favourite chocolate cake for birthdays. We would stuff clean, wrapped coins into the bottom layer so that every person got a coin. My dad always asked, "Is there money in the cake?" It wasn't a birthday without money in the cake.

You can prepare this in even the most basic of kitchens. If you are on holidays, just bring along some foil pans to bake it in. Don't be afraid to buy a tub of prepared icing if necessary.

CAKE

1 - 16-ounce (500 gram) box
    chocolate cake mix
3 eggs
½ cup (125 mL) vegetable oil
1⅓ cups (325 mL) water

CHOCOLATE ICING

1 cup (250 mL) soft butter

2 cups (500 mL) icing sugar
1 cup (250 mL) cocoa powder
2 to 4 tablespoons (30 to 60 mL)
    strong coffee

12 to 14 coins, washed and
    wrapped in wax paper
Coloured sprinkles or
    other candy for decoration
Candles

Prepare the cake mix according to package directions. If you want to put money in your cake, it is easiest to bake two 8- or 9-inch (1.2 or 1.5 L) rounds. Cool the cakes on a rack.

Prepare the icing. Place butter, icing sugar and cocoa in the bowl of a food processor fitted with a metal blade. Pulse the mixture, turning the machine on and off several times. Slowly add the coffee through the feed tube. Mix until the icing is spreading consistency. Transfer the icing to a bowl.

Lay 1 cake layer on a piece of wax paper. Spread about one-quarter of the icing over the cake layer. Vertically stuff the coins into the cake, working around the outside of the cake. You want to be sure that every serving gets a coin. Place the second layer on top of the first. With the remaining icing, generously ice the top and sides of the cake. With 1 hand on the bottom of the cake, slide the wax paper out from under the cake and place the cake on a serving plate. Decorate the top of the cake with sprinkles or other candy. This is where you can let small children express their artistic talent. Let them go wild. Keep the cake in the fridge until ready to serve. Don't forget the candles. Serve with vanilla ice cream.

Apricot and Pecan Fruit Cake

The quantities given here make 4 large loaves.
You can make smaller loaves if you wish,
just cut down the cooking time.

*I have been making this cake for about 30 years, more and more of them
each year. We used to sell them in December at* The Cooking Company, *wrapped in floral foil and cellophane bags. In the past few years I have
sold them at a craft fair in one of our local high schools. With the cooler
temperatures in December, I usually have a box of them in the back of my
car to sell to those who ask for them.*

*My kids don't eat this cake, although I know many who do. They always
say it wouldn't be Christmas without the smell of fruit cake filling the house.
It also wouldn't be Christmas cake season without a box of apricots or dates
set in front of them with a pair of scissors when they sit down to watch TV.*

*I have never before given out this recipe, although many have asked for
it. Last year I made over 350 cakes and developed bursitis in my elbow from
stirring the batter. So now I'm passing on the recipe!*

1 pound butter (500g), room temperature
2¼ (560 mL) cups golden brown sugar
1 cup (250 mL) honey
9 eggs, room temperature
4 cups (1 L) flour
2 teaspoons (10 mL) baking powder
2 teaspoons (10 mL) cinnamon
1 teaspoon (5 mL) allspice
½ teaspoon (2 mL) salt
6 cups (1.5 L) dried apricots, sliced in
    three pieces

5 cups (1.25 L) pecans
3½ cups (875 mL) pitted dates,
    sliced in three
3 cups (750 mL) golden raisins
1 cup (250 mL) apricot nectar
½ cup (125 mL) light cream
2 tablespoons (30 mL) lemon juice

1 cup (250 mL) brandy
¼ cup (60 mL) Triple Sec or Cointreau

Line 4 – 9 x 5-inch (23 cm x 13 cm) loaf pans with wax paper or parchment
paper. Grease the paper with butter. Preheat oven to 280F (140C).

Combine flour, baking powder, cinnamon, allspice and salt in a medium
bowl. In another very large bowl or tub combine apricots, pecans, dates

and raisins. Add half the flour and spice mixture to the dried fruit. Stir well to coat all the fruit with the flour. Reserve the remaining flour mixture.

In a measuring cup, combine apricot nectar, cream and lemon juice.

In the bowl of an electric mixer, beat the butter and brown sugar together. Add the honey, mixing well. Add the eggs, one at a time, beating well after each addition. Add the liquid ingredients and mix just until incorporated. Add the reserved flour and spice mixture and stir until all the flour is combined. Pour this mixture over the dried fruit and mix well by hand until all the batter is incorporated into the fruit. Divide the batter among the four prepared pans. Bake for 2½ to 3 hours until a skewer inserted in the middle comes out clean.

Cool cakes on a rack for 15-20 minutes. Combine brandy and Triple Sec in a measuring cup. Spoon the brandy mixture over the cakes, dividing it evenly. Cool the cakes completely. Wrap in wax paper and then in foil. Store the cakes in the fridge.

Cakes are best made at least three weeks before eating. They will keep for more than a year in the fridge.

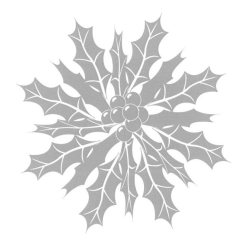

muffins & breakfasts

The trick with any muffins is not to overmix them. When adding the wet ingredients to the dry, fold gently just until the ingredients are incorporated. Fill the muffin tins almost to the top to get big muffins with high tops.

Apple Streusel Muffins

Makes 9 muffins

I don't think you can go wrong with a muffin recipe that calls for buttermilk and butter. These muffins are really easy to put together; they make a nice addition to a brunch table and are a great after-school snack.

STREUSEL TOPPING

¼ cup (60 mL) flour
¼ cup (60 mL) brown sugar
½ teaspoon (2 mL) cinnamon
2 tablespoons (30 mL) cold butter
2 tablespoons (30 mL) chopped pecans (optional)

MUFFINS

1½ cups (375 mL) all-purpose flour
1 teaspoon (5 mL) baking powder
½ teaspoon (2 mL) baking soda
1 teaspoon (5 mL) cinnamon
½ teaspoon (2 mL) allspice
1 cup (250 mL) brown sugar, packed
2 eggs
¼ cup (60 mL) butter, melted and cooled
1 cup (250 mL) buttermilk
1 large apple, peeled, cored and diced small

Preheat oven to 375F (190C). Butter 9 muffin tins or line with paper muffin cups.

Make the streusel topping. Put the flour, brown sugar and cinnamon in a small bowl. Cut in the butter with a pastry cutter. Add the chopped nuts and set aside.

For the muffins, combine the flour, baking powder, baking soda, cinnamon, allspice and brown sugar in a medium bowl. Stir well. In another bowl, beat the eggs; add the butter and buttermilk. Mix well. Add the chopped apple to the wet mixture and pour the wet mixture over the dry mixture. Mix gently just until flour is incorporated. Spoon the mixture into the muffin tins, filling to the top. Gently press about 1 tablespoon (15 mL) streusel topping onto each muffin.

Bake for about 25 minutes, until golden brown and firm on top.

Gingerbread Muffins

Makes 15 muffins

2¾ cups (675 mL) all-purpose flour
2½ teaspoons (12 mL) baking soda
1 heaping tablespoon (15 mL) ground ginger
1 teaspoon (5 mL) cinnamon
⅛ teaspoon (½ mL) cloves
½ teaspoon (2 mL) salt
½ cup (125 mL) butter, room temperature
½ cup (125 mL) sugar
2 large eggs

¾ cup (175 mL) fancy molasses
1⅓ cups (325 mL) cold water

LEMON GLAZE

3 tablespoons (45 mL) fresh lemon juice
3 tablespoons (45 mL) sugar

Preheat oven to 350F (180C). Butter 15 muffin tins or line with paper muffin cups.

Mix together flour, baking soda, ginger, cinnamon, cloves and salt in a medium bowl. In another bowl, cream together butter and sugar. Add 1 egg at a time, mixing well after each addition. Add molasses. Add half of the dry ingredients and slowly mix until almost combined. Add all the water, mix it in a bit and then add the remaining dry ingredients; mix lightly. Spoon the dough into muffin cups, filling them almost to the top. Bake about 25 minutes until they are firm in the middle when you touch them.

While the muffins are baking, combine lemon juice and sugar in a micro-wave container or in a small saucepan. Heat for about a minute to dissolve the sugar. Brush muffins with warm glaze when they are hot from the oven. For a real treat serve with whipped cream.

Blueberry Muffins

Makes 12 muffins

These muffins were a staple at The Cooking Company. *They are great with homemade jam.*

2½ cups (625 mL) all-purpose flour
1 cup (250 mL) sugar
1 tablespoon (15 mL) baking powder
1 cup (250 mL) blueberries, fresh or frozen

2 eggs
1¼ cup (310 mL) buttermilk
½ cup (125 mL) melted butter, cooled

Preheat oven to 350F (180C). Butter 12 muffin tins or line with paper muffin cups.

Combine flour, sugar and baking powder in a medium bowl. Add blueberries. In another bowl, combine eggs, buttermilk and melted butter; mix well. Gently add wet ingredients to dry ingredients. Mix to incorporate flour, being careful not to overmix. Spoon mixture into muffin tins, filling to the top. Bake 30 to 35 minutes, until lightly golden.

Rhubarb and Orange Muffins

Makes 9 muffins

In the spring when the rhubarb is new and fresh, buy some extra and chop it up and freeze it, unprocessed, in bags. You can use it in these tangy muffins as well as in fruit crumble.

2 cups (500 mL) all-purpose flour
¾ cup (175 mL) sugar
2 teaspoons (10 mL) baking powder
½ teaspoon (2 mL) baking soda
½ teaspoon (2 mL) salt
1 egg
Zest of 1 orange
¼ cup (60 mL) orange juice
¼ cup (60 mL) sunflower oil
¾ cup (175 mL) buttermilk
1 cup (250 mL) finely diced rhubarb

Preheat oven to 350F (180C). Butter 9 muffin tins or line with paper muffin cups.

In a medium bowl combine the flour, sugar, baking powder, baking soda and salt. In another bowl beat the egg; add the orange zest, orange juice, oil, buttermilk and diced rhubarb. Pour wet ingredients over dry ingredients. Mix gently, just until all the flour is incorporated. Do not overmix. Spoon batter into prepared muffin cups, filling to the top. Bake about 25 minutes or until muffins are firm in the centre.

Lemon Cream Cheese Muffins

Makes 7 muffins

These muffins are nice and moist because they are brushed with a lemon glaze when they are hot. If you don't already have one, invest in a silicone pastry brush. You can use it for sweet and savoury items, because it washes up very well and doesn't hold flavours.

1½ cups (375 mL) all-purpose flour
1½ teaspoons (7 mL) baking soda
½ teaspoon (2 mL) salt
½ cup (125 mL) plus 2 tablespoons (30 mL) sugar
3 tablespoons (45 mL) cream cheese, chilled
1 egg
¼ cup (60 mL) sunflower oil
½ cup (125 mL) buttermilk
Zest and juice of 1 large lemon

Preheat oven to 350F (180C). Butter 7 muffin tins or line with paper muffin cups.

In a medium bowl, combine flour, baking soda, salt and ½ cup (125 mL) sugar. Add chilled cream cheese and cut into flour mixture with a pastry cutter or a fork. Beat the egg in a medium bowl and add the oil, buttermilk, lemon zest and 1 tablespoon (15 mL) of the lemon juice. Reserve the remaining juice for the glaze. Add the wet ingredients to the dry. Mix gently, being careful not to overmix. Spoon the batter into prepared muffin tins, filling them to the top. Bake muffins 20 to 25 minutes, until golden around the edges.

While muffins are baking, combine remaining sugar and lemon juice (about 2 tablespoons/30 mL) in a microwaveable cup with high sides so that it doesn't boil over. Heat for 1 minute until sugar is dissolved. Alternatively, heat the glaze in a small saucepan on the stove over medium heat for 1 minute. Brush hot glaze over muffins when they come out of the oven.

SILICONE PASTRY BRUSHES are available in any kitchen shop. You can put them in the dishwasher and they don't hold the flavour of the last food you used them for. If you are brushing lemon glaze over a loaf, you don't want to use a traditional pastry brush that had garlic butter on it last time it was used.

Banana Pecan Muffins

Makes 10 muffins

The easiest way to mash bananas is with a pastry cutter. Be careful not to overmix the batter or the muffins will become tough. Children love these muffins with peanut butter.

2 cups (500 mL) flour
½ cup (125 mL) brown sugar, packed
¼ cup (60 mL) wheat germ
1½ teaspoons (7 mL) baking powder
1 teaspoon (5 mL) baking soda

¼ cup (60 mL) chopped pecans (optional)
2 ripe bananas
1 egg
⅓ cup (75 mL) butter, melted and cooled
1 cup (250 mL) buttermilk

Preheat oven to 350F (180C). Butter 10 muffin tins or line with paper muffin cups.

Combine the flour, brown sugar, wheat germ, baking powder and baking soda in a medium bowl. Add the chopped pecans. In another bowl, mash the bananas. Add the egg, melted butter and the buttermilk. Mix to combine. Pour the wet ingredients over the dry ingredients and mix lightly until just combined. Do not overmix. Spoon batter into prepared muffin cups, filling them to the top. Bake 20 to 25 minutes, until muffins are firm in the centre.

Frozen Fruit Yogurt Smoothie

Serves 1

I keep a bag of mixed fruit, usually berries and peaches, in my freezer so they are handy to make smoothies at any time of year.

½ cup (125 mL) frozen mixed fruit
½ banana
½ cup (125 mL) yogurt, plain, vanilla or fruit
¾ cup (175 mL) orange juice

Combine mixed fruit, banana, yogurt and orange juice in a blender and purée until smooth.

Double this recipe and pour the leftovers into popsicle holders and freeze.

Buttermilk Scones

Makes 8 to 10 scones

Scones are the perfect after-school snack, but be sure to make enough for breakfast the next day. They are quick to mix together and as they don't need much time in the oven you can prepare them fresh in the morning, if you prefer.

2 cups (500 mL) all-purpose flour
2 tablespoons (30 mL) sugar
2 teaspoons (10 mL) baking powder
1 teaspoon (5 mL) baking soda

¼ teaspoon (1 mL) salt
5 tablespoons (75 mL) cold butter
⅔ cup (150 mL) buttermilk
1 egg

Preheat oven to 400F (200C).

Combine flour, sugar, baking powder, baking soda and salt in a medium bowl. Cut in the butter using a pastry cutter. In a small bowl beat together the buttermilk and the egg. Add to the flour mixture and mix to absorb flour. Turn out onto a lightly floured surface and knead gently. Roll or press out the dough to ½ inch (1 cm) thickness. Cut out scones using a 2½- or 3-inch (7 to 10 cm) cookie cutter and transfer to an ungreased baking sheet. Gather together the remaining dough and repeat. If you don't have cookie cutters, you can flatten the dough into a circle and cut it, like a pie, into triangles. Separate the triangles on the baking sheet before baking.

Bake the scones 14 to 16 minutes, until puffed and golden.

Granola

Makes 12 to 14 cups

I have been making this granola for years. It's my old standby. My mum started making it in the 1970s and we have shared this recipe with others many times. Don't forget that the raisins are not cooked with the granola as they will burn: they are added after the granola is baked.

¾ cup (175 mL) sunflower oil
1 cup (250 mL) honey
8 cups (2 L) rolled oats
½ cup (125 mL) flax seeds
½ cup (125 mL) sesame seeds
1 cup (250 mL) sunflower seeds

1 cup (250 mL) cashew pieces,
  raw unsalted
1 cup (250 mL) peanuts, raw unsalted
¾ cup (175 mL) wheat germ
¾ cup (175 mL) milk powder
1 cup (250 mL) Thompson seedless raisins

Preheat oven to 325F (160C). Line 2 baking sheets with parchment paper, making sure it comes up the sides of the pan.

Combine oil and honey in a microwave-proof container and heat 2 minutes on high. Alternatively, heat the mixture on the stove in a small saucepan until warm.

Mix together the rolled oats, flax seeds, sesame seeds, sunflower seeds, cashews, peanuts, wheat germ and milk powder in a large bowl. Do not add the raisins until after the granola is cooked.

Add warmed oil and honey. Stir well to moisten. Spread granola evenly over the 2 prepared pans. There should not be any empty space on the baking sheets, and the granola should not be any thicker than ¾ inch (1.5 cm) deep. Bake 20 to 40 minutes, until golden, stirring 2 or 3 times with a spatula as it cooks. Don't let it burn.

When cooked, take out of the oven and let pans cool on racks without mixing. This is what makes granola nice and lumpy. When cool, transfer to a bowl and stir in raisins.

Store the granola in sealed containers. It will keep in the fridge for several weeks or in the freezer for several months.

Cranberry Pumpkin Granola

Makes 14 to 16 cups

This is a slightly updated version of my original granola recipe. It has some spices in it and is partly sweetened with applesauce. You can put any seeds, nuts or fruit in granola: the trick is to have the correct proportions of wet and dry. The dry ingredients should be completely moistened, but not soggy. The other important thing is that the granola must be mixed several times during cooking; it takes about 40 minutes to cook and you have to watch it carefully. Burnt granola is really not very good!

8 cups (2 L) rolled oats
2 cups (500 mL) raw pumpkin seeds
2 cups (500 mL) whole raw almonds, skins on
⅔ cup (150 mL) flax seeds
1½ cup (375 mL) raw sunflower seeds
⅔ cup (150 mL) sesame seeds
1½ cup (375 mL) raw shelled peanuts
1 tablespoon (15 mL) ground cinnamon
2 teaspoons (10 mL) ground ginger
1 teaspoon (5 mL) salt
¾ cup (175 mL) honey
¾ cup (175 mL) sunflower oil
½ cup (125 mL) unsweetened applesauce
2 cups dried cranberries or raisins

Preheat oven to 300F (150C). Line 2 large baking sheets with parchment paper.

In a large bowl, combine the rolled oats, pumpkin seeds, almonds, flax seeds, sunflower seeds, sesame seeds, peanuts, cinnamon, ginger and salt and mix well. Heat honey in a large glass measuring cup for about 1 minute in the microwave. Add oil and applesauce. Alternatively, heat the honey, oil and apple sauce in a small saucepan on the stove until warm. Pour the honey mixture over the dry ingredients and stir well.

Spread granola evenly over the 2 baking sheets, being sure to spread it out to all the corners. Place in oven and set timer for 20 minutes. Remove from oven and mix granola around on the baking sheets. The granola at the edges of the pans cooks faster so mix the outside parts into the centre and push the centre parts to the outside. Return to oven and set timer for an additional 10 minutes. Continue mixing granola and returning to oven until granola is evenly cooked but not burnt. It should not be soft or soggy. Remove from oven and cool. Sprinkle cranberries or raisins over top. Transfer cooled granola to an airtight container. It keeps well for several weeks in the pantry or fridge and can also be frozen.

Banana Bread with Chocolate Chips

Makes 1 large loaf

You don't have to put chocolate chips in this banana bread, but they sure make it taste good.

½ cup (125 mL) soft butter
1 cup (250 mL) sugar
2 eggs
1 cup (250 mL) mashed ripe banana
2 tablespoons (30 mL) lemon juice
1 teaspoon (5 mL) vanilla
1¾ cups (425 mL) all-purpose flour
1 teaspoon (5 mL) baking soda
1 teaspoon (5 mL) baking powder
1 cup (250 mL) chocolate chips

Preheat oven to 350F (180C). Butter a 9 x 5 x 2½-inch (2 L) loaf pan.

Cream the butter and add the sugar, beating until light and fluffy. Add 1 egg at a time, beating well after each addition. Stir in mashed banana, lemon juice and vanilla. Add flour, baking soda, baking powder and chocolate chips all at once. Gently stir or fold in dry ingredients, just until combined. Be careful not to overmix. Pour into the prepared loaf pan and bake about one hour, until loaf is firm to the touch on top. Cool on a rack.

Pancake and Waffle Mix

Serves 4

When I was growing up, the food floor of Woodward's store in Vancouver sold a pancake mix made in part with whole wheat flour. We missed it when they went out of business. This recipe is a pretty good copy. You can double the recipe and keep it in airtight jars in the pantry. I would rather add real eggs and milk to this homemade pancake mix than use a store-bought mix that calls for water.

2 cups (500 mL) all-purpose flour
1 cup (250 mL) whole wheat flour
2 tablespoons (30 mL) baking powder
2 tablespoons (30 mL) sugar
1 teaspoon (5 mL) salt

Combine all-purpose flour, whole wheat flour, baking powder, sugar and salt and store in a jar in the pantry until ready to use.

To prepare pancakes or waffles, combine 1 cup (250 mL) mix with 1 egg and 1 cup (250 mL) buttermilk. You can substitute regular milk or use half buttermilk and half regular milk.

For pancakes, heat about 1 tablespoon (15 mL) butter in a large skillet on medium-high heat. Pour in pancake mix, making them any size you like. Flip the pancakes when they are golden brown.

For waffles, heat waffle iron. Brush a small amount of butter or oil onto the griddle. Pour in some waffle mix. Close the lid and cook until the waffles are golden brown.

Serve pancakes and waffles with soft butter and warm maple syrup or jam.

christmas dinner

Also on our Christmas menu

On Christmas Day we have a traditional turkey dinner with all the trimmings. Usually there are 12 people at our feast but sometimes as many as 30 sit around card tables on folding chairs, piano benches and whatever we can find. Some of the guests bring food and we always have an assortment of Christmas baking on hand, some baked by us, others by friends.

Preparing Christmas dinner shouldn't be a daunting task, especially as there are many things that can be made in advance.

MENU

Red Pepper Jelly & Cream Cheese
on Water Crackers
Sundried Tomato & Goat Cheese
Spread & Crackers

✿

Roast Turkey with Celery
& Almond Stuffing
Gravy
Cranberry Orange Sauce

✿

Scalloped Oysters

✿

Make-Ahead Mashed Potatoes
Shaved Brussels Sprouts
Glazed Carrots
Frozen Peas
Gratin of Root Vegetables

✿

Bûche de Noël
Steamed Carrot Pudding
Assorted Christmas Baking

Organizing Your Time for Christmas Dinner

Here's a schedule to help you organize your food preparation for Christmas dinner. You can begin up to two weeks ahead so that you're ready and relaxed on the big day itself.

TWO WEEKS AHEAD, OR MORE

- Make and freeze Turkey Gravy
- Make and freeze Bûche de Noël
- Make Cranberry Orange Sauce

ONE WEEK AHEAD

- Prepare Nana McLennan's Steamed Carrot Pudding
- Prepare Brandy Hard Sauce
- Prepare the Make-Ahead Mashed Potatoes (if freezing)

TWO DAYS AHEAD

- Prepare the Gratin of Root Vegetables
- Prepare the Make-Ahead Mashed Potatoes (if not freezing)
- Prepare Celery and Almond Stuffing for Turkey

ONE DAY AHEAD

- Prepare Scalloped Oysters
- Prepare Glazed Carrots
- Prepare Shaved Brussels Sprouts

CHRISTMAS DAY

- Roast the Turkey

How to Make Gravy Ahead of Time

Makes 4 or 5 cups (1 to 1.25 L), enough to serve 6 to 8

Can you ever have enough gravy? Don't forget you'll need some for the hot turkey sandwiches on Boxing Day.

Turkey gravy is usually made after the bird comes out of the oven. If you don't want this last-minute task, you can prepare the gravy in advance by using fat and drippings saved from a turkey roasted earlier in the year. Another idea is to roast some chickens a few weeks before Christmas and use the drippings to make and freeze gravy. Combine it with some onion gravy (see page 164) so that you have enough for all the guests.

Turkey fat
Turkey drippings
Broth made from turkey neck (see page 174)
Extra broth
Cooking juice from potatoes
Flour
Salt and freshly ground pepper
Browning and seasoning sauce

From a turkey or chicken roasted earlier, pour the drippings from the roasting pan into a glass measuring cup and chill in the fridge overnight. The next day, remove the fat from the top and freeze the drippings and fat separately, well labelled with the date.

Using this fat and drippings, you can make gravy 1 or 2 days ahead of Christmas, or even 1 or 2 weeks ahead if you freeze it.

Measure the fat and place in a saucepan over low heat. As the fat heats up, slowly whisk in some flour, about 1 tablespoon (15 mL) at a time. You should have equal quantities of fat to flour (if you have about ½ cup (125 mL) of fat, you will use about ½ cup (125 mL) of flour). Be sure to cook the fat and flour mixture for several minutes, stirring, until it just begins to turn a shade darker in colour. Begin by adding about 4 cups (1 L) of liquid, a combination of broth and the water in which you boiled pota-toes. Add the drippings and slowly bring the gravy to a boil, whisking fre-quently. Add more liquid as required to get the gravy the consistency you like. Season with salt and pepper to taste. For extra seasoning and colour add 1 to 2 teaspoons of browning and seasoning sauce. Cool the gravy and refrigerate or freeze.

If this has not made enough gravy you may need to add ready-made gravy, using the onion gravy recipe or a good quality gravy from your local food market.

Onion Gravy

Makes about 6 cups/1.5 L

This gravy can be made 1 or 2 days ahead and reheated on low before serving. It can also be frozen for several months. I often combine some of this with my turkey gravy when I need really big quantities for Christmas.

4 cups (1 L) finely chopped onions (about 2 to 3 large)
½ cup (125 mL) butter
2 large garlic cloves, mashed
⅓ cup (75 mL) flour
5 cups (1.25 L) chicken broth
1 teaspoon (5 mL) browning and seasoning sauce
2 tablespoons (30 mL) brandy (optional)
¼ cup (60 mL) light cream (optional)
Salt and freshly ground pepper

In a medium-sized saucepan with a heavy bottom, melt the butter and add the chopped onions. Cook the onions over medium to medium-low heat for about 20 minutes, until they turn golden brown. Add the garlic and cook for about 1 minute. Add the flour and cook for 1 minute more. Add the broth and bring the gravy to a boil, stirring often. Add the browning and seasoning sauce and brandy if using. Simmer about 10 minutes. Add the cream if using and check for seasoning. The amount of salt and pepper necessary will depend on how salty the broth is.

Bûche de Noël (Christmas Log)   Serves 15 to 20

*Bûche de Noël is a tradition for many families. I particularly like
this recipe because it can be made several weeks in advance and frozen.
A sprinkling of icing sugar makes it look like a snow-covered log.*

CAKE

5 large eggs
1⅓ cup (325 mL) sugar
½ cup (125 mL) cold black espresso or
   1 tablespoon (15 mL) instant coffee
   granules dissolved in ½ cup (125 mL)
   hot water
1½ teaspoon (7 mL) vanilla
1½ cups (375 mL) flour
½ cup (125 mL) finely chopped roasted
   hazelnuts
1½ teaspoon (7 mL) baking powder
¼ teaspoon (1 mL) salt

2 to 3 tablespoons (30 to 45 mL) icing sugar

COFFEE-CREAM FILLING

1 cup (250 mL) whipping cream
3 tablespoons (45 mL) icing sugar
1 tablespoon (15 mL) instant coffee granules
   dissolved in 1 tablespoon (15 mL) hot water

CHOCOLATE-COFFEE ICING

1 cup (250 mL) soft butter
2 cups (500 mL) icing sugar
1 cup (250 mL) cocoa
1 to 2 tablespoons (15 to 30 mL) strong
   coffee or 1 tablespoon (15 mL) instant
   coffee granules dissolved in 1 tablespoon
   (15 mL) hot water

To prepare the cake, preheat oven to 375F (190C). Line a 15 x 11 x 1-inch (38 x 28
x 2 cm) jelly roll pan with wax paper or parchment paper and grease the paper.

With an electric mixer beat the eggs 3 to 4 minutes until light in colour. Slowly
add the sugar and continue to beat 1 to 2 more minutes. Add the coffee and
vanilla and mix gently. Stop the mixer and remove the mixing blade. Add the flour,
hazelnuts, baking powder and salt to the egg mixture and gently fold ingredients
together until all the flour is incorporated. Scrape onto jelly roll pan, spreading evenly
to the corners. Bake 15 to 20 minutes, until golden brown and springy to the touch.

Lay a clean tea towel out on the counter. Sprinkle top of cake with icing sugar
and turn the hot cake out onto tea towel. Carefully remove the parchment or
wax paper. Fold the flap of tea towel over the cake and gently roll up the cake
at the long side, to make a long thin roll. Cool completely on a rack.

Meanwhile prepare the coffee cream filling. Using a cold bowl and cold beaters
beat the cream until soft peaks form. Add the icing sugar and cold dissolved coffee;
mix to combine. Keep in fridge until ready to use.

To make chocolate-coffee icing, place butter, icing sugar and cocoa in the bowl of a food processor fitted with a metal blade. Pulse several times to combine. Slowly add coffee through feed tube until icing is a good spreading consistency. Keep at room temperature until ready to ice the cake.

When the cake is completely cool, carefully unroll it. Spread the coffee-cream filling over the inside of the cake. Carefully roll it back up. Using a sharp serrated knife cut off about one-third of the cake at a 45-degree angle. Place the longest part of the cake on a serving platter. Place the shorter piece on the platter at an angle so that it resembles a branch growing out of a log. Ice the cake all over with the chocolate-coffee icing. Try to spread the icing the length of the log and make wavy lines in it with a fork to resemble bark. Cover with wax paper, then cover tightly with plastic wrap and freeze.

Remove the cake from the freezer 24 hours ahead of time and put it in the fridge. Just before serving, carefully unwrap the cake, sprinkle with icing sugar and decorate with a sprig of holly.

Cranberry Orange Sauce

Makes about 2½ cups (625 mL)

Any cranberries left over from this recipe will freeze well in a sealed bag. Later you can throw a few of them into a fresh fruit crumble. If you wish to give this sauce as a gift, process it in a boiling water bath so it won't have to be kept in the fridge. (See instructions for making jam, pages 176–177.)

¾ cup (175 mL) sugar
½ cup (125 mL) water
Zest and juice of 1 orange

¼ teaspoon (1 mL) ground cinnamon
¼ cup (60 mL) port
3 cups (750 mL) fresh cranberries

In a medium heavy saucepan, combine sugar, water, orange zest and juice, cinnamon and port. Bring to a boil. As soon as the mixture boils add the cranberries. Cook about 10 minutes until the berries pop and the sauce thickens. When cool, transfer to a glass jar with tight-fitting lid and store in the fridge.

Nana McLennan's Carrot Pudding

Serves 12 to 14

Some of us are not very fond of traditional Christmas puddings but this one is light and tasty. There is something nice about the tradition of lighting the pudding at the table just before it is served. Many years ago, when my cousin Sarah was about nine years old, she wanted to light the pudding. The burning brandy spilled onto the tablecloth and burned a big hole in it. We never let Sarah forget her eagerness to take part in this Christmas tradition because my mum still has the tablecloth and you can see the spot where it was mended.

PUDDING

1 cup (250 mL) flour
1 teaspoon (5 mL) baking soda
½ teaspoon (2 mL) ground cinnamon
½ teaspoon (2 mL) ground allspice
½ teaspoon (2 mL) ground nutmeg
¼ teaspoon (1 mL) ground cloves
1 cup (250 mL) grated carrot
1 cup (250 mL) grated potato
1 cup (250 mL) grated apple

1 cup (250 mL) raisins or dried cranberries
½ cup (125 mL) butter, room temperature
1 cup (250 mL) brown sugar

BRANDY HARD SAUCE

½ cup (125 mL) unsalted butter,
    room temperature
1½ cups (375 mL) icing sugar
2 tablespoons (30 mL) brandy

To prepare the pudding, you will need a small (6 cup/1.5 L) deep ceramic bowl in which to steam the pudding and a pot with a rack on the bottom of it. (If you don't have a rack, place several screw-on canning rings in a single layer on the bottom of the pot.) You will also need some parchment paper, foil and kitchen string.

Turn the ceramic bowl over onto the parchment paper and trace a circle the same size as the top of the bowl. Cut out the circle of paper. Butter the ceramic bowl.

In a small bowl combine the flour with the baking soda, cinnamon, allspice, nutmeg and cloves. Set aside.

In a large bowl combine the carrot, potato, apple and raisins or cranberries. Toss this mixture with ⅓ of the flour and spice mixture.

In another bowl beat the butter and add the brown sugar. Beat for 1 to 2 minutes until light and fluffy. Add the butter mixture and the remaining flour mixture to the carrot mixture. Mix together well with your hands. Transfer the pudding to the ceramic bowl. Place the round of parchment paper over the top, pressing down lightly. Cover the top of the bowl with another large piece of parchment paper and a large piece of foil. Tie some string around the top rim of the bowl to secure the paper and the foil.

Put the rack on the bottom of the steaming pot and add about 3 inches (7.5 cm) water. Place the pudding bowl on the rack and cover pot with a lid. Bring the water to a simmer and then turn it down to low or medium low heat. The water should simmer lightly for a full 2½ hours. You will need to check the water level frequently so that it doesn't boil dry. Top it up from time to time. Cool the pudding on a rack and refrigerate.

To prepare the brandy hard sauce, in a small bowl beat butter for several minutes until light and fluffy. It should appear a few shades lighter in colour. Add the icing sugar ½ cup (125 mL) at a time, beating well after each addition. Stir in the brandy. This sauce can be made several days in advance.

At the beginning of Christmas dinner, take the hard sauce out of the fridge to bring it up to room temperature. Reheat the pudding for 10 to 15 minutes at medium power in the microwave or by putting it back in the pot with the rack and steaming it for 30 minutes. Turn pudding onto serving dish.

Warm 2 or 3 tablespoons (30 to 45 mL) brandy. Turn out the lights and have a sprig of holly ready as a garnish. With the warm brandy in a heatproof glass carefully light it on fire in the glass and quickly pour it over the pudding. Garnish with holly. Children love the bright blue flame, but it's better if they just watch and don't touch!

Serve with brandy hard sauce.

Celery and Almond Stuffing for Turkey

Makes enough stuffing for a large, 16- to 22-pound (7 to 10 kg), turkey

This is the stuffing my mum always made when we had roast turkey. Although I have tried other recipes, I always go back to this one. If you have more stuffing than space in the turkey, or if there are vegetarian guests, place extra stuffing in a baking dish and bake for 30 to 40 minutes along with the turkey.

Try to buy your bread a few days before making the stuffing or ask for some day-old bread at the bakery. I usually go through my freezer and pull out any bread or buns that need to be used up. Making the stuffing a day ahead allows it to be nice and cold before it goes into the bird. It is important for the stuffing to be cold to prevent bacteria from growing before the turkey goes in the oven.

1½ cups (375 mL) slivered almonds
2 to 3 loaves stale bread or assorted buns or about 12 cups (3 L) fresh bread crumbs or chunks
2 large onions
1 head celery

½ cup (125 mL) butter
2 tablespoons (30 mL) chopped fresh sage
1 tablespoon (15 mL) chopped fresh rosemary
2 teaspoons (10 mL) salt
1 teaspoon (5 mL) freshly ground pepper

Set oven to 350F (180C). Toast the almonds, watching them carefully so that they don't burn. Toast for about 5 to 7 minutes until light golden. Cool.

Prepare the bread crumbs in one of two ways: you can dice the bread with a sharp serrated knife, or you can break it into 2- to 3-inch (5 to 7 cm) chunks and chop them in the food processor, using the on/off pulse. It's O.K. to have some big chunks. Place the breadcrumbs in a large bowl.

Chop the onions. Peel the outside strings off the celery using a vegetable peeler and chop the celery in ½-inch (1 cm) chunks.

Melt the butter in a large skillet. Add the onions and celery. Sauté over medium heat until they begin to soften, 10 to 15 minutes. Add the sage, rosemary and salt and pepper. Pour the vegetables and butter over the breadcrumbs and stir well. Add the almonds. If stuffing seems too dry, add another ¼ cup (60 mL) melted butter.

Cover and chill well.

Scalloped Oysters

Serves 8 to 12

Our tradition of having scalloped oysters with Christmas dinner goes back longer than I can remember. The recipe comes from my mum's family. Along with her sister Judy, we were able to decipher the recipe after looking over several greasy recipe cards. We only make a small amount of oysters, as not everybody eats them. They are rich and delicious.

1 pint (500 grams) oysters in juice
1½ cups (375 mL) crushed premium saltine crackers
½ cup (125 mL) butter, melted
2 teaspoons (10 mL) lemon juice
½ teaspoon each salt and freshly ground pepper
¾ cup (175 mL) light cream
1 tablespoon (15 mL) sherry
1 teaspoon (5 mL) Worcestershire sauce
2 to 3 shakes hot sauce

Butter a small 3- to 4-cup (1 L) ovenproof gratin pan.

Drain the oysters in a sieve set over a bowl; reserve the juice.

Combine the cracker crumbs with the melted butter, lemon juice and salt and pepper. In another bowl combine the cream with ½ cup (125 mL) of the reserved oyster juice, sherry, Worcestershire sauce and hot sauce.

Sprinkle half of the cracker crumb mixture in the bottom of the buttered dish. Arrange the drained oysters in a single layer over the top. Pour the cream mixture over the oysters. Sprinkle the remaining crumbs over the top.

Oysters can be prepared one day ahead. Cover with plastic wrap and refrigerate.

Bake the oysters at 350F (180C) for 40 minutes. They should be bubbly around the edges.

Cooking the Turkey

Serves 15 to 20

For Christmas dinner I always order a fresh free range or organic turkey. Pick it up from the butcher or grocer a day or two before Christmas. If you have to buy a frozen bird, be sure to thaw it completely, following instructions on the packaging.

Remove the neck from the turkey cavity and use it to make the broth for the gravy. Get this done a day or two ahead if you can.

Once the turkey is cooked it is important to let it sit, covered, for at least 30 minutes before carving. Plan your time well. Take the fresh turkey out of the fridge about 1 hour before you want to put it in the oven. Cleaning it and stuffing it will take time. Remember that you want it to come out of the oven 30 to 60 minutes before you eat, so plan accordingly.

FOR THE TURKEY	EQUIPMENT	FOR BROTH	FOR GRAVY
1 – 16- to 22-pound (7 to 10 kg) turkey	Butcher's string	1 turkey neck	Fat
Celery Almond Stuffing	Small skewers	1 onion, quartered	Drippings
Salt and freshly ground pepper	Aluminum foil	1 carrot, chopped	Flour
3 to 4 tablespoons (45 to 60 mL) butter	Turkey baster	1 stalk celery, chopped	Broth
	Meat thermometer	1 bay leaf	Potato juice
	Turkey lifter	6 to 10 peppercorns	Salt and freshly ground pepper
			Browning and seasoning sauce

Preheat oven to 325F (160C). Set the oven rack towards the bottom. Turn on convection if you have it.

Place about 1 teaspoon (5 mL) of salt and ½ teaspoon (2 mL) pepper in a small bowl and have it ready to sprinkle on the clean turkey. Clean your kitchen sink and lay out some clean tea towels or paper towel beside the sink. Remove the turkey from its bag in the sink. Discard the bag. Keep the neck for the broth.

Rinse the turkey inside and out with cold water. Drain and transfer to towels. Dry the bird inside and out. Sprinkle the inside of the turkey with about one-third of the salt and pepper mixture. Turn the turkey over and sprinkle the smaller neck cavity with salt and pepper. Spoon some of the stuffing into this cavity. Bring the excess skin over the stuffing and secure it with a skewer. Turn the turkey back over and stuff the larger cavity with remaining stuffing. Tie the wings to the bird with string. Tie some more string around the drumsticks to hold them in place.

If you have a roasting pan with a rack that curves upwards, that should work to hold the turkey in place without using string. If you have a chain turkey lifter (available in cook shops or hardware stores), lay it inside the roasting pan. This will make it much easier to get the bird from the roasting pan to the platter. Place the turkey in the roasting pan. Rub about 3 to 4 tablespoons (45 to 60 mL) of butter all over the bird. Sprinkle with remaining salt and pepper mixture. Cover the top with a large piece of foil to prevent the turkey from browning too quickly. Place in the oven. A stuffed turkey of this size will take 4 to 4½ hours to cook. In a convection oven it will take slightly less time.

Put the thermometer into the breast or leg of the turkey after about 2½ to 3 hours. I like to move the thermometer occasionally to get an accurate reading. After the first 2 hours, remove the foil from the turkey. Save the foil to cover the bird when it comes out of the oven. Start basting the bird after about 1½ hours and continue to baste every 30 minutes or so. The turkey is done when the temperature reads 170 to 175F (75 to 80C). The temperature of the stuffing should be at least 160F (70C). It is important to let the turkey rest for at least 30 minutes before slicing as this seals in the juices. When the turkey comes out of the oven, put any vegetables and side dishes in for heating.

When you move the turkey from the roasting pan to the carving platter, you will need some extra hands. This is when a chain turkey lifter in the pan makes the turkey easier to move. If you do not have a turkey lifter, you will first need to loosen the turkey from the sides and bottom of the roasting pan or rack. Be sure that it isn't stuck anywhere. Have the platter right beside the roasting pan. Large metal or wooden spoons may help. When you have transferred the turkey, cover it with the foil and then a clean tea towel or a bigger towel if the bird is really large. Be sure that the towel doesn't rest right on the platter, or it will soak up the juices that you want to add to your gravy.

To Make Gravy on Christmas Day

Put the turkey neck, onion, carrot, celery, bay leaf and peppercorns in a large pot. Cover with 12 to 16 cups (3 to 4 L) water. Bring to a boil. Turn down the heat and simmer for 30 minutes. Cool, strain and chill if you have time. This way any fat particles can be removed from the top of the broth.

Pour all the drippings from the roasting pan into a glass measuring cup. Let them sit until the fat separates from the juices. If you have already made your gravy in advance, chill these drippings in the fridge overnight. The next day, separate the fat from the actual drippings and freeze them separately, well labelled.

If you have any reserved potato juice from making mashed potatoes you can use it too.

Using the turkey baster, take the fat off the top of the turkey juices and return it to the roasting pan. Place the roasting pan over 2 burners and set the heat to medium-low. As the fat heats up, slowly whisk in some flour, about 1 tablespoon (15 mL) at a time. You should have equal quantities of fat to flour. If you had about ½ cup (125 mL) fat, you will use about ½ cup (125 mL) flour. Be sure to cook the fat and flour mixture for several minutes until it just begins to turn a shade darker in colour. Begin by adding about 4 cups (1 L) liquid. Use a combination of both broth and potato juice. Slowly bring the gravy to a boil, whisking frequently. Add more liquid as required to get the gravy the consistency that you like. Season with salt and pepper. Pour any juices that have accumulated around the turkey into the gravy. I like to add 1 teaspoon (5 mL) or two of browning and seasoning sauce to my gravy, a little trick my mum taught me. You can find it at your grocer with the bouillon cubes. I use browning and seasoning sauce to add extra colour and flavour. Transfer the gravy to one or two jugs for serving.

Final Preparations

When the turkey comes out of the oven put the potatoes and gratin of root vegetables in. They will take 45 to 50 minutes at 350F (180C).

Bake the scalloped oysters at 350F (180C) for about 40 minutes. Put some water on to boil for the peas. The peas will only take about 5 minutes to cook. Drain them, reserving the cooking water for your gravy if needed, and stir in a dollop of butter and some salt. Reheat the carrots in the microwave for about 5 minutes on high heat. Warm the Brussels sprouts in a skillet over low heat.

Set up any tables if needed. Light the candles. Open the wine. Put water on the tables. Put cranberry sauce on the tables.

To Carve the Turkey

Get everything ready for carving. You will need a sharp knife and a large carving fork. Have a large plate ready for the sliced turkey and a bowl for the stuffing. Start by carving the breast into thin slices and place them on the plate. Remove the drumsticks and cut the meat off them. Spoon the stuffing out of the cavity and transfer it to a bowl. Have a clean spoon ready for serving.

After Dinner

Remove all meat to a container and store carcass and meat separately in the fridge.

Turkey Soup

Serves 12

Some people roast turkey at Christmas just so they can eat turkey soup a few days later. Here's how to make it.

TURKEY BROTH

1 turkey carcass
1 to 2 onions, skin on, quartered
2 carrots, roughly chopped
2 stalks celery, roughly chopped
2 bay leaves
12 to 20 peppercorns

TURKEY SOUP

1 to 2 onions, diced
2 to 3 peeled carrots, diced
2 to 3 celery stalks, diced
3 tablespoons (45 mL) butter
12 cups (3 L) turkey broth
1 to 2 garlic cloves, mashed
2 to 3 cups (500 to 750 mL) chopped turkey meat
½ cup (125 mL) rice or barley or 1 cup (250 mL) pasta
Salt and freshly ground pepper

To prepare the broth, place the turkey carcass and neck in a very large stock pot along with onions, carrots, celery, bay leaves, peppercorns and enough water to cover. Bring to a boil, turn down heat and simmer, covered, 30 to 40 minutes.

Strain into a large bowl and chill overnight to solidify any fat particles. Remove the fat. If you want a really clean broth, strain it through cheesecloth.

To make the soup, in a large pot sauté the diced onions, carrots and celery in butter until soft. Add garlic and cook for a minute or two. Add turkey broth, topping up the quantity of homemade turkey broth with commercially prepared chicken broth if necessary; bring to a boil. Turn down heat. Add turkey meat and either rice, barley or pasta. Season the soup well with salt and pepper. Simmer, covered, until rice or pasta is cooked, 30 to 40 minutes. The soup freezes well.

making jam

I make my own jam every summer for us to eat all through the year. It is not difficult to make but much easier if you have the right tools.

Equipment

An enamel canning pot with a rack inside. These are not expensive and are available at any hardware store.

Canning jars with screw on lids, readily available in the summer months, but usually throughout the year as well. The jars and screw on lids are reusable but you need to buy new tops each time, as they cannot be used more than once. The jars usually come with plain gold lids but you can buy decorative lids which look really nice, especially if you plan on taking some jars as gifts.

A plastic stick with a magnet on the end, also available with the canning tools. This is used to pull the sterile metal lids out of boiling water, just before they are placed on the hot jam jars.

A large heavy pot for cooking the fruit, the largest and heaviest you have (Le Creuset pots are ideal).

Blender (optional) and **glass measuring cup** for transferring hot jam to blender.

Paper towels for wiping rims of jars after they are filled.

Preparation

Wash the jars in hot soapy water and rinse well. Wash a few more than you think you might need, with a combination of 1-cup (250-mL) and 2-cup (500-mL) jars.

Sterilize the clean jars by placing them on a baking sheet on the bottom rack of a pre-heated 250F (120C) oven. They will need at least 30 minutes in the oven.

Fill the enamel canning pot about three-quarters full of water. Cover and set over medium heat to bring it to the boil.

Sterilize the two-piece canning lids by covering them with cold water in a saucepan and bringing to a boil over high heat. Boil for about five minutes. Turn off the heat and let them sit in the water until the jam is ready.

Making the Jam

Boil the jam, following one of the recipes below.

Transfer jam to blender jar using a glass measuring cup. Don't fill the blender more than one-third to one-half full. The jam is very hot and it is best to use rubber gloves in case any spurts out the top when you turn the blender on. Purée the jam for about 5 seconds. (Blending the jam is optional).

Pour the hot jam into the hot jars from the oven. Never fill the jars to the top. Leave about ½- to ¾-inch (1 to 1.5 cm) space.

Clean the rims of the jars with paper towel dipped in boiling water. If there is any jam on the rims, the jars won't seal properly.

Remove the round metal tops from the water with the magnet and dab them dry on clean paper towel. Gently set them on the jars.

Remove the screw tops from the water with the magnet and screw one onto each lid, being careful not to tighten them up too much.

Process the jars in boiling water. Be sure the water in the enamel canning pot is at a full boil. Place the jars in the canning rack and carefully lower the rack into the water. The jars should have at least 1 inch (2 cm) water covering them. Have the kettle full of boiling water ready to top up the canning pot as needed. Bring the water back up to the boil and process the jars in the boiling water 20 to 25 minutes.

Remove the rack from the pot, using oven mitts. Without touching the tops, place the jars on a clean tea towel. Within a few minutes you should hear the tops pop down. This is when all the air is pulled out of the jar; the tops will look slightly concave.

When the jars are cool, gently tap the tops to be sure they are sealed. If the jar is not sealed the top will be slightly convex and it will sound hollow. If this is the case, the jam is still perfectly edible, but you will have to keep that jar in the fridge. Well-sealed jars can be stored in the pantry.

Allow the jam to cool completely in the jars before storing, usually about 12 hours. When the jars are cool, label them with the contents and the date. You can store them in the boxes the jars came in. Label the boxes with the date too.

It is well worth buying all kinds of berries at the height of the season and freezing them to make jam whenever you have time, or to enjoy fruit desserts all winter long. Lay the berries in a single layer on baking sheets lined with wax paper. Freeze until they are solid, then put them in re-sealable bags or empty ice cream buckets and keep frozen until you need them.

Raspberry Jam

Makes about 7 – 1-cup (250 mL) jars

I don't use pectin for my jam, just the berries and sugar. This is a simple recipe from Gordon's grandmother, Nanny Mackie.

8 cups (2 L) raspberries
6 cups (1.5 L) sugar

Wash the jars and set them in the oven to sterilize, following the instructions for making jam (pages 176–177).

Use a large pot with a very heavy bottom. Put the raspberries in the pot and mash them with a potato masher. Turn the heat to high and bring the raspberries to a boil, stirring frequently; boil for 1 full minute then add the sugar. Bring the mixture back up to a full boil, stirring frequently. Time the boiling for 3 minutes. Remove the jam from the heat and skim any foam from the top.

Ladle some jam into the jar of a blender, filling about one-third full. Purée the jam for about 5 seconds. Pour it into the hot jars. Repeat using all the jam. Place the lids on the jars. Place the jars in the canner and boil for 20 to 25 minutes. Remove the jars from the canner and let them cool completely, about 12 hours. Label the jars and store in a cool dark place.

Strawberry Rhubarb Jam

Makes about 11 – 1-cup (250 mL) jars

Read the instructions for making jam (page 176) It isn't necessary to blend Strawberry Rhubarb Jam because the fruit cooks down so much.
*   You will need a very large heavy-bottomed pot for this amount of jam. The jam boils up the sides of the pan and you don't want it to boil over. If you don't have a large pot, cook the jam in two batches or halve the recipe.*

10 cups (2.5 L) strawberries, washed, hulled and halved
7 cups (1.75 L) rhubarb, washed and cut in ½-inch (1 cm) dice
9 cups (2.25L) sugar

Combine strawberries, rhubarb and sugar in a large bowl. Let stand at room temperature for 2 to 3 hours or until sugar is dissolved.

Sterilize the jars and lids following the instructions for making jam (page 176). Fill the canning pot ¾ full of water so that it is ready to bring to the boil as the jam is cooking.

Place 2 or 3 small plates in the freezer to test the consistency of the jam as it cooks.

Put the strawberry mixture in a very large pot, scraping all the sugar out of the bowl. Bring the jam to a full rolling boil. It will boil up very high. Turn down the heat slightly, maintaining the full boil. Stir frequently so that the jam does not stick to the bottom of the pot. Boil the jam for 25 to 30 minutes.

Test the thickness of the jam by spooning about a teaspoonful onto a cold plate from the freezer. When the jam seems thick enough to spread on toast, turn off the heat. Skim the foam off the top of the jam.

Follow the instructions for filling jars, processing and cooling (pages 176–177).

Blackberry Jam   Makes about 7 – 1-cup (250 mL) jars

In August I pick blackberries on Salt Spring Island. I usually don't want to make the jam right away, using up the weekend, so I freeze them for later. They are good not only for jam but for fruit crumble and other desserts.

8 cups (2 L) blackberries
6 cups (1.5 L) sugar

Wash the jars and set them in the oven to sterilize, following the instructions for making jam (pages 176–177).

Use a large pot with a very heavy bottom. Put the blackberries in the pot and mash them with a potato masher. Turn the heat to high and bring the blackberries to a boil, stirring frequently, and boil for 1 full minute. After boiling for a minute, add the sugar. Bring the mixture back up to a full boil, stirring frequently. Time the boiling for 2 minutes. Remove the jam from the heat and skim any foam from the top.

Ladle some jam into the jar of a blender, filling about one-third full. Purée the jam for about 5 seconds. Pour it into the hot jars. Repeat using all the jam. Place the lids on the jars. Place the jars in the canner and boil for 20 to 25 minutes. Remove the jars from the canner and let them cool completely, about 12 hours. Label the jars and store in a cool dark place.

Spiced Red Currants

Makes 7 or 8 – 1-cup (250 mL) jars

*My mum and her sister, my Aunt Judy, remember driving out to
Lulu Island (now known as Richmond) with their mother to buy red
currants. When they got home, the sisters had to remove all the
currants from the stems; they would try to invite unsuspecting
friends over to make the job go faster.*

10 cups (2.5 L) red currants
5½ cups (1.25 L) sugar
1½ tablespoons (22 mL) ground cloves
2 tablespoons (30 mL) ground cinnamon
½ cup (125 mL) cider vinegar

Wash the jars and set them in the oven to sterilize, following the
instructions for making jam (pages 176–177). Boil the lids in a pot
of water.

To remove red currants from the stem, hold the stem at the top and run
the tines of a fork down the length of it so that the currants can fall off
into a bowl. Rinse the currants and drain well on baking sheets lined
with paper towel.

Combine red currants, sugar and spices in a large saucepan with
a heavy bottom. Slowly bring the mixture to a boil; this should take
about 15 minutes. Stir the currants frequently.

When the mixture comes to a full boil, turn down to simmer and let
it bubble for about 30 minutes. Add the vinegar and continue to cook,
stirring, for another 15 to 20 minutes.

The spiced currants should thicken up and start to stick to the
bottom of the pan. When this happens they are ready to can. Follow
the instructions for canning in making jam (see pages 176–177), omitting
the blending and boiling the jars for 20 to 25 minutes. Cool completely
and label the jars.

Community Meals

Casseroles to feed 80–100 people

For several years I have been involved in preparing a community meal through our local church. The free lunch program was started in 2002 by two dedicated parishioners. The hot meal consists of a nutritious casserole, two hot vegetables, green salad, fresh bread, juice, ice cream and goodies baked by volunteers.

The program is run by volunteers from all around our community. Although the church provides the kitchen and venue, only some of the volunteers are parishioners. There are cook teams who prepare the casseroles, usually the day before; other volunteers shop for fresh produce and beverages. Some come in the morning to set tables and arrange flowers. Others come for a few hours to serve, while some tough it out in the dish pit until all the dishes are washed and put away. Getting volunteers for this program has never been a problem: it is surprising how many people are happy to come out and help, knowing they are making a real difference.

Many local businesses help fund this meal. We also accept donations at the door, though these don't make up much of the funding. One year we held a fundraising dinner. We served a community meal in the evening to invited guests willing to pay $75 per plate. We charged for wine and had prizes to raffle off. At first we cooked in an old church kitchen but after some fundraising we were able to upgrade it to commercial standards. If you wish to have a similar program in your community, there are a few recipes here to get you started. If your facilities are limited, why not serve soup and sandwiches? Some of the soup recipes earlier in this book can be multiplied to serve larger numbers.

My job for the community meal is organizing the cook teams and providing the recipes. Typically there are three or four people on a team. We prepare enough food for about 100 meals and usually have enough food to send some home with people.

For vegetables, we prepare about 20 pounds (9K) of carrots, peeled, sliced and steamed for 5-10 minutes in large pots with 3-4 inches of boiling water. We steam cauliflower or broccoli, cut in flowerets, in the same way, and add 6 thinly sliced onions and 8 red peppers that have been sautéed in butter and oil. The vegetables are kept warm in steam tables or on heating trays. Salad is usually a combination of romaine and baby greens, simply tossed with vinaigrette dressing.

Participating in a community meal is a rewarding experience for all involved, an added bonus for the volunteers being the camaraderie that develops between them. Guests come from the immediate neighbourhood and the wider community: our sidewalk sign says "All are welcome." One of our guests once remarked "I always like coming to this meal because I can tell that here the food is cooked with love."

BASIC EQUIPMENT

- 6 large roasting pans, metal or foil
- Parchment paper
- 2 large heavy-bottomed pots
- 2 large skillets
- Large colander
- 2 large stainless bowls
- Chopping boards and sharp knives

HEATING DIRECTIONS

For each of these recipes you will need 6 large foil or metal roasting pans. Heat casseroles at 350F–375F (180C–190C) for 60 to 90 minutes. The internal temperature of the casseroles should measure 165F (74C). Uncover towards the end to brown the tops.

Chicken Tetrazzini

Serves 80 to 100

This dish is really popular with both guests and volunteers. It also freezes well.

20 pounds (9.5 kg) boneless skinless chicken thighs
6 to 8 heads celery, washed and chopped
10 to 12 onions, chopped
2 heads garlic, peeled and chopped
¾ cup (175 mL) oil
3 - 100-ounce (3 L) cans mushrooms, drained
5 pounds (2.5 kg) macaroni or other pasta
2 pounds (1 kg) butter

4 cups (1 L) flour
32 cups (8 L) whole milk
2 - 48-ounce (1.36 L) cans chicken broth
4 - 48-ounce (1.36 L) cans condensed cream of mushroom soup

4 pounds (2 kg) Mozzarella cheese
1½ pounds (750 grams) grated Parmesan cheese
Salt and pepper

Preheat oven to 350F (180C). Line some baking pans with foil and divide the chicken between the pans. Season with salt and pepper and cover with foil. Cook chicken 30 to 40 minutes. Be sure that the chicken is cooked through. Cool slightly and slice into bite-size pieces.

Bring 2 large pots of water to the boil for the pasta. Salt the water. Cook the pasta 8 to 10 minutes. Drain and rinse with cold water so it does not stick together.

Using 2 heavy-bottom pots, melt 1 pound (500 grams) butter in each pot over medium-low heat. When butter is melted, add 2 cups (500 mL) flour to each pot. Stir constantly and cook about 5 minutes. Add 1 jug (4 L) of milk and 1 can of chicken stock to each pot. Over medium heat bring the sauce to a simmer, stirring often. Keep a close eye on the sauce as it can burn easily. It will take 30 to 45 minutes to come to a simmer, then add mushroom soup, 2 cans per pot, and boil gently for a few minutes.

Sauté the onions in 2 large skillets with about ¼ cup (60 mL) oil in each pan. Add minced garlic for the last 5 minutes of cooking. Transfer to a large container. Sauté celery in the same 2 pans with about 2 tablespoons (30 mL) oil for each pan.

Place the 6 pans on the counter, line with parchment and grease well. Divide the cooked pasta between the 6 pans. Divide the cooked chicken, mushrooms, onions, garlic and celery between the 6 pans. Sprinkle each pan with about 2 teaspoons (10 mL) pepper. Divide the sauce between the pans, mixing well. Be generous with the sauce: these casseroles need to be saucy. Taste for seasoning and add salt if needed. Combine Mozzarella and Parmesan cheeses. Sprinkle over top of each casserole. Cover casseroles with parchment and foil and refrigerate or freeze as required. Heat as described on page 182.

Beef Stroganoff

Serves 80 to 100

*This casserole freezes well because the mushroom soup acts
as a stabilizer.*

10 large onions, chopped
3 heads garlic, chopped
20 pounds (9.5 kg) lean ground beef
1¼ cups (325 mL) flour
2 - 100-ounce (3 L) cans mushrooms
  pieces, drained

6 - 48-ounce (1.36 L) cans condensed
  cream of mushroom soup
8 cups (2 L) chicken broth
4 tablespoons (60 mL) pepper
Salt to taste
26 cups (6.5 L) sour cream
10 pounds (4.5 kg) penne pasta

Bring 2 very large pots of salted water to the boil and cook penne,
divided between the 2 pots. Drain and rinse with cold water to prevent
sticking.

Brown beef and onions in 2 or 3 very large pots. When beef is browned
and there are no longer any pink bits, add garlic and sauté 5 minutes more.
Add flour, mix well and cook 5 minutes. Add mushrooms, mushroom soup,
broth and seasonings and slowly bring to boil over medium heat. Be careful not to burn the bottom of the pots. Simmer the sauce for 10 minutes.
Add sour cream and heat but do not boil.

Set the 6 foil or metal pans out on the counter. Line with parchment paper
and generously grease them. Divide the cooked pasta and meat mixture
between the pans. Mix well. Cool on counter for about 30 minutes.
Cover with parchment and then foil and refrigerate or freeze
as required. Heat as described on page 182.

Sausage and Penne Casserole

Serves 80 to 100

This dish is wonderful because you don't have to pre-cook the pasta. Be sure to use diced tomatoes.

18 pounds (8.5 kg) honey garlic or other sausage
14 large onions, diced
2 heads garlic, peeled and chopped
⅓ cup (75 mL) olive oil
⅓ cup (75 mL) Italian seasoning or a combination or basil and oregano
2½ teaspoons (12 mL) crushed red pepper flakes
1 cup (250 mL) cornstarch

32 cups (8 L) whole milk
4 – 100-ounce (3 L) cans diced tomatoes
1 – 48-ounce (1.36 L) can chicken broth
Salt and freshly ground pepper
30 cups (4 kg) penne pasta
1 – 24-ounce (750 gram) bag grated Parmesan cheese
1 – 24-ounce (750 gram) bag grated Mozzarella cheese

Line the 6 pans with parchment and grease well.

Cut sausage into ½-inch (1 cm) pieces. Sauté sausage in large skillets on medium-high heat, until browned and cooked through. Divide cooked sausage between the 6 pans.

Sauté onions in olive oil in skillets until soft and beginning to brown. Add chopped garlic and continue cooking another 5 minutes. Divide the onion mixture among the 6 pans. Dissolve the cornstarch in a cup of the milk. In a large stock pot heat the milk, tomatoes, stock, cornstarch and seasonings over medium heat. Bring the mixture slowly to a boil, stirring constantly so that it doesn't burn. The sauce should thicken somewhat.

Add 5 cups (1.25 L) penne (raw) to each pan. Divide the Parmesan between the 6 pans. Spoon the sauce evenly over each casserole. The mixture will be quite runny, which is good, as the raw pasta will absorb the excess sauce. Taste for seasoning and add salt and pepper if needed. Allow the casseroles to cool on the counter for about 20 to 30 minutes before covering with parchment and then foil and refrigerating. Sprinkle Mozzarella cheese on top before heating. Heat as described on page 182.

Tuna and Penne Casserole   Serves 80 to 100

This tuna casserole is creamy and flavourful. The breadcrumb topping keeps the casserole moist inside.

10 large onions, chopped
4 large heads celery, chopped
½ cup (125 mL) oil
1 – 100-ounce (3 L) can mushrooms, drained
2 pounds (1 kg) butter
4 cups (1 L) flour
½ cup (125 mL) soy sauce
16 cups (4 L) chicken or vegetable broth
16 cups (4 L) whole milk

1 tablespoon (15 mL) freshly ground pepper
4 – 4-pound (1.88 kg) cans tuna packed in water
5 to 6 cups (1 kg) frozen peas
5 pounds (2.6 kg) penne pasta
6 cups (1.5 L) fresh breadcrumbs made from bread or buns
3 pounds (1.5 kg) Cheddar cheese, grated
1 cup (250 mL) chopped parsley

Line the 6 pans with parchment and grease well.

Cook pasta in 2 large pots in boiling salted water, drain, rinse with cold water, drain again and divide among the 6 prepared pans.

Begin making the white sauce. Divide the 2 pounds (1 kg) butter between 2 large heavy-bottomed saucepans. Melt slowly. When the butter is melted add 2 cups (500 mL) flour to each pan. Cook over medium heat for about 5 minutes without browning. Add the stock and milk, divided between the 2 pans. Bring to boil slowly without burning. This will take 30 to 45 minutes. If you try to rush it using higher heat, the sauce will burn. Season the sauce with pepper and soy sauce. Add some salt only if needed. Be sure that the sauce bubbles for at least 15 seconds.

Divide onions and celery between 2 large skillets that have ¼ cup (60 mL) oil in each. Sauté onion with celery until soft but not brown. Divide onion mixture between the 6 pans.

Drain mushrooms and divide among the pans. Drain tuna and divide among the pans. Divide frozen peas among the pans.

When the sauce has come to the boil, divide among the pans. Stir all the ingredients together inside the pans.

Make breadcrumbs using a food processor. Grate cheese. In a bowl combine crumbs, cheese and parsley. Sprinkle topping over each casserole. Cover with parchment and then foil. Refrigerate or freeze as required. Heat as described on page 182.

Macaroni and Cheese with Ham

Serves 80 to 100

If the onions are cold from the fridge, there will be fewer tears while cutting.

10 pounds (4.5 kg) macaroni
2 pounds (1 kg) butter
10 large onions, chopped
2 heads garlic, peeled and finely chopped
3 tablespoons (45 mL) dry mustard powder
1 tablespoon (15 mL) cayenne
4 cups (1 L) flour
20 cups (5 L) chicken broth

24 cups (6 L) whole milk
10 pounds (4.5 kg) medium or sharp
   Cheddar cheese, grated
1 – 6½-pound (3 kg) bag frozen peas
2 – 4- to 5-pound (2 to 2.5 kg) boneless
   Black Forest hams, cubed
40 slices white bread, ripped
1¼ cups (325 mL) butter, melted

Fill 2 very large stock pots with water and add 1 tablespoon (15 mL) salt to each pot and bring to a boil. Cook half the macaroni in each pot until al dente, about 5 to 7 minutes. Drain, rinse with cold water and set aside.

Using 2 heavy-bottomed pots, melt 1 pound (500 grams) butter in each pot over medium-low heat. Add the onions, divided, and sauté over medium-high heat until just starting to brown. Add garlic, mustard and cayenne, divided between the 2 pots, and cook until fragrant, about 1 minute. Add half the flour to each pot and cook, stirring constantly, for 2 to 3 minutes. Slowly whisk half the chicken broth and half milk into each pot; bring to a simmer and cook, stirring often, until large bubbles form on the surface and the mixture is slightly thickened. This will take 30 to 45 minutes. Don't rush it or the sauce will burn. Turn off the heat. Stir half the grated cheese into each pot gradually until completely melted. Season the sauce with salt and pepper.

Line the 6 foil or metal pans with parchment and grease well. Divide the cooked macaroni among the 6 pans. Add the frozen peas and cubed ham. Divide the sauce between the 6 pans and stir the ingredients well. Keep in mind that it should be quite saucy as the pasta absorbs the sauce.

Pulse the bread in a food processor until coarsely ground. In a large bowl, combine the breadcrumbs and the melted butter. Sprinkle the breadcrumb mixture over the 6 pans of macaroni. Cover with parchment paper and foil and refrigerate. Heat as described on page 182.

Index

ACKNOWLEDGEMENTS

"May I have the recipe?" Numerous family and friends have asked this question over the years and this book is the result. These are the people who got me started recording my recipes and I thank them. You know who you are.

In particular, I thank my publisher, Joan Coldwell, whose guidance and advice over the past two years helped me navigate the uncharted waters of cookbook writing. My friend Jill Lambert helped me remain focused and kept my head above water through the entire process. Without the encouragement and enthusiasm of Liz Jacobson, Linda Yorke, Corinne Jefferson, Joan Love and many other family and friends, this book may have floundered in the waves. Ann-Marie Metten's editing of each chapter and her professionalism were of invaluable assistance.